AI in Law

Discover how Artificial Intelligence is transforming the legal profession—from research and contracts to compliance and justice. Equip yourself with the tools to thrive in the AI-driven future of law.

Written by

ERIC LEBOUTHILLIER

AcraSolution | 2025 1st Edition
www.acrasolution.com

Preface

Who this book is for

This book is written for lawyers, paralegals, law students, compliance officers, and business professionals who want to understand how Artificial Intelligence is reshaping the legal landscape. Whether you are an experienced attorney looking to streamline case research, a law student exploring the future of practice, or a corporate leader navigating regulatory compliance, this book provides clear, practical insights without unnecessary jargon.

What to expect from this book

Readers will gain a solid foundation in the core AI technologies applied to law, explore how AI is transforming legal research, contract analysis, and litigation, and learn how compliance monitoring is being automated worldwide. Each chapter blends real-world applications with critical discussion of risks, ethics, and future possibilities—helping you separate hype from reality. By the end, you'll have the knowledge to harness AI responsibly in your legal work and stay ahead of the curve in an evolving profession.

LEGAL DISCLAIMER

This publication is intended solely for informational and educational purposes. It does not constitute legal, financial, medical, or professional advice. The content is not a substitute for consultation with qualified experts or licensed professionals in the relevant fields.

Portions of this work have been created or assisted by artificial intelligence (AI) tools. While every reasonable effort has been made to review, fact-check, and edit the content for clarity and accuracy, AI-generated information may occasionally contain errors, omissions, or generalized statements. The author and publisher do not guarantee the accuracy, completeness, or reliability of the information provided.

Readers are strongly encouraged to seek independent advice tailored to their personal circumstances from qualified legal, financial, healthcare, or compliance professionals before making decisions or taking action based on this content.

References to specific products, services, companies, websites, or technologies do not imply endorsement or affiliation unless explicitly stated. All trademarks and brand names mentioned remain the property of their respective owners.

The author and publisher disclaim any liability, loss, or risk incurred directly or indirectly from the use or misuse of this publication. This includes, but is not limited to, damages of any kind — including incidental, special, or consequential — arising out of the reliance on the material presented.

All references to laws, regulations, security standards, or industry guidelines are intended for general awareness only and may not reflect the most current legal developments. This publication is not intended to create, and receipt does not constitute, a client relationship with the author, publisher, or any affiliated entity.

By reading, accessing, or applying the content in this publication, you agree to do so at your own risk. If you do not accept these terms, you are advised to discontinue use of this material immediately.

Table of Contents

CHAPTER 1

Introduction to AI in the Legal Field

The Rise of AI Across Industries and Why Law Is No Exception

Artificial Intelligence (AI) is no longer a futuristic concept—it is an active force reshaping industries at breathtaking speed. From healthcare to finance, from manufacturing to creative work, AI has become an essential driver of efficiency, accuracy, and innovation. The legal profession, often perceived as conservative and resistant to change, is now entering this transformation. While law has unique characteristics that make the adoption of AI more complex, it is not immune to the global wave of technological evolution.

The rise of AI in law is not simply about adopting new tools; it represents a fundamental shift in how legal knowledge is accessed, applied, and delivered. To understand why, we must first explore how AI has already redefined other industries—and why its entry into the legal field was only a matter of time.

AI's Proven Impact Across Key Industries

AI first demonstrated its power in industries where data volume and decision-making speed are critical. In healthcare, machine learning models analyze medical images with accuracy rivaling top radiologists, catching early signs of disease that humans might overlook. In finance, AI-driven algorithms detect fraud in real time, process millions of transactions per second, and even manage investment portfolios with predictive insights.

Even creative industries are not exempt. Generative AI now produces music, art, and written content, challenging assumptions about human exclusivity in creativity. Meanwhile, in transportation, self-driving systems analyze thousands of variables simultaneously to make split-second driving decisions.

The common thread across these examples is clear: AI excels in environments where information is vast, rules are complex, and the cost of error is high. By that measure, the legal field—with its endless volumes of statutes, precedents, contracts, and regulatory requirements—is a natural candidate for AI transformation.

Why Law Has Been Slow to Change

Despite AI's demonstrated potential, law has historically been cautious in embracing innovation. Several reasons explain this hesitation:

1. **Tradition and Precedent** – Law is built on precedent, stability, and continuity. Rapid technological change can feel at odds with these values.
2. **High Stakes** – Legal outcomes affect lives, businesses, and justice itself. The margin for error is far smaller than in other industries.
3. **Complexity of Legal Language** – Unlike financial transactions or medical scans, legal texts are nuanced, context-dependent, and resistant to standardization.
4. **Ethical and Professional Concerns** – Lawyers are bound by strict codes of conduct and client confidentiality obligations, raising concerns about delegating tasks to machines.

Yet, these very challenges highlight why AI's arrival in law is inevitable. The legal system produces more information than any professional can reasonably process, and clients increasingly demand faster, more cost-effective services. AI offers solutions to pressures that human expertise alone cannot resolve.

Why Law Can No Longer Resist AI

Three forces make AI adoption in law not only likely but necessary:

1. **Data Overload** – The volume of legal data—court decisions, statutes, regulations, contracts—grows exponentially. AI's ability to parse and analyze vast datasets far outpaces human capacity.
2. **Client Expectations** – Businesses and individuals expect legal services that are faster, cheaper, and more accessible. AI provides the efficiency that modern clients demand.
3. **Competitive Advantage** – Law firms and in-house legal teams that adopt AI gain an edge in accuracy, speed, and insight. Those who resist risk falling behind in both capability and reputation.

A practical illustration can be found in e-discovery during litigation. A decade ago, legal teams manually reviewed millions of emails and documents at tremendous cost. Today, AI tools can filter irrelevant content, highlight patterns, and surface key evidence within hours. What once required armies of junior associates is now automated with remarkable precision—saving both time and resources.

The Global Shift Toward AI-Enabled Law

AI adoption in law is not confined to a few pioneering firms. Around the world, governments, courts, and regulatory bodies are experimenting with AI-driven tools. For instance, Estonia has piloted an AI system to help resolve small claims disputes. In the United States, AI-powered platforms already assist in contract analysis and due diligence for corporate transactions. China has even deployed AI-driven "smart courts" where algorithms assist judges in managing caseloads.

These developments signal a broader truth: law cannot remain isolated from the technological transformations reshaping every other industry. If healthcare, finance, and even creative fields can embrace AI responsibly, the legal sector—arguably the most information-dense profession—has both the need and the opportunity to do the same.

Key Takeaway

AI is not arriving in the legal profession in isolation—it is part of a global, cross-industry evolution driven by data, speed, and efficiency. The very qualities that make law complex—its reliance on massive bodies of text, precedent, and intricate reasoning—are the same qualities that make it ripe for AI assistance. Law may have been slow to embrace change, but the pressures of data overload, client expectations, and global competition ensure that AI is no longer a distant possibility. It is here, and its role in law will only expand.

Historical Evolution: From Digital Research Tools to Predictive Analytics

The integration of technology into law did not happen overnight. Long before today's AI-powered platforms, the legal profession began its digital journey with tools that automated the simplest but most time-consuming tasks. This gradual evolution—from basic databases to advanced predictive systems—shows how the foundations for AI in law were laid over decades. Understanding this progression not only highlights how far the profession has come but also clarifies why predictive analytics represents a natural next step in legal innovation.

The First Wave: Digital Legal Research

In the 1970s and 1980s, the first digital research platforms emerged. Services like **LexisNexis** and **Westlaw** transformed legal research by digitizing statutes, case law, and secondary sources. Before this shift, lawyers and clerks spent countless hours leafing through physical law reports and libraries to find relevant precedents.

With digital databases, search efficiency improved dramatically. Instead of scanning hundreds of pages manually, lawyers could now query large collections of texts using keywords. The profession recognized these tools as revolutionary because they reduced research time from days to hours, allowing lawyers to focus more on legal reasoning and less on clerical work.

Yet, keyword search had limitations. A single term could return thousands of irrelevant results, and the subtle nuances of legal language often escaped simple search algorithms. The next stage of evolution would tackle these shortcomings.

The Second Wave: Enhanced Search and Analytics

By the late 1990s and early 2000s, improvements in natural language processing (NLP) and metadata tagging brought more sophistication to legal research. Search tools evolved from simple keyword queries to **semantic search**, which attempted to understand context and meaning rather than just matching words.

For example, a lawyer researching "duty of care in negligence" could now retrieve cases that used different wording but addressed the same legal principle. Advanced filtering options allowed researchers to prioritize results by jurisdiction, time frame, or relevance.

This era also marked the rise of **analytics dashboards**. Legal databases began offering visualizations of how often certain cases were cited, how judges ruled in specific circumstances, and how legal doctrines evolved over time. This shift foreshadowed the predictive tools we see today by turning raw information into structured insights.

The Third Wave: Machine Learning in Legal Practice

The early 2010s saw the rise of machine learning in law. Instead of simply retrieving documents, AI-driven platforms began to **learn from past cases and user behavior**. Tools such as **Ravel Law** and **Lex Machina** pioneered this approach by analyzing patterns in judicial decisions, litigation strategies, and case outcomes.

For example, Lex Machina could show that a particular judge historically ruled in favor of patent holders in 70% of cases. This data gave lawyers powerful strategic insights—helping them assess risks, predict case outcomes, and tailor arguments more effectively.

Similarly, e-discovery tools began using machine learning to prioritize relevant documents in massive litigation cases. Instead of reviewing millions of files manually, AI systems "learned" from attorney decisions and applied those patterns to filter out irrelevant material. This not only accelerated the process but also reduced costs significantly.

The Current Wave: Predictive Analytics

The most recent phase of evolution is **predictive analytics**—AI systems that go beyond past data to forecast future legal outcomes. These tools leverage massive datasets of prior rulings, judge tendencies, and legal arguments to estimate the probability of success in litigation or negotiation.

For instance, platforms can now predict the likelihood of a case being dismissed at summary judgment, or the probable damages awarded in a specific type of lawsuit. In transactional law, predictive systems evaluate risks hidden in contracts, flagging unusual clauses or compliance gaps before they become costly disputes.

Predictive analytics doesn't replace human judgment—it augments it. Lawyers still interpret and contextualize these insights, but with a stronger evidence-based foundation. This evolution reflects the legal profession's shift from **reactive research** (finding what the law says) to **proactive strategy** (anticipating how the law will be applied).

Key Takeaway

The history of legal technology shows a clear trajectory: from digitization (making information accessible), to advanced search (making information usable), to machine learning (making information actionable), and finally to predictive analytics (making information strategic). Each stage built upon the previous one, preparing the legal profession for today's AI-powered tools.

Far from being a sudden disruption, AI in law is the product of decades of incremental progress. What began as a way to replace heavy books with searchable databases has now evolved into systems capable of anticipating legal outcomes. This journey reveals a crucial truth: AI is not an external force imposed on law, but the natural continuation of its technological evolution.

Key Drivers for AI Adoption in Legal Practices

The legal profession has always balanced tradition with innovation. While courts, statutes, and precedents form a centuries-old foundation, the practice of law does not exist in isolation. It operates within the same economic, technological, and social forces that shape every industry. The recent acceleration of AI adoption in law is not just a matter of convenience—it is the result of powerful drivers pushing firms, corporations, and courts toward transformation.

Driver 1: The Explosion of Legal Data

The volume of legal information has reached unprecedented levels. Courts generate thousands of new rulings every week, legislatures continuously pass and amend laws, and regulatory bodies publish an ever-growing web of compliance requirements.

For example, multinational corporations must track data privacy laws across multiple jurisdictions, each with different obligations and penalties. A single merger may involve reviewing hundreds of contracts, thousands of emails, and terabytes of communication data.

No human team, no matter how skilled, can efficiently process this scale of information without technological assistance. AI thrives in precisely this environment—it can parse, categorize, and highlight relevant patterns across vast datasets in seconds.

Driver 2: Client Demands for Efficiency and Transparency

Clients are no longer willing to pay for inefficiency. In the past, law firms billed hours for tasks like manual document review or basic research. Today, corporate clients demand faster turnaround times, cost predictability, and measurable value.

AI-powered tools directly address these expectations by automating repetitive tasks such as contract review, due diligence, and e-discovery. When a client sees that an AI-driven system can analyze thousands of documents at a fraction of the cost and time, it becomes difficult for firms to justify older, slower methods.

This shift is not just about cost—it's about transparency. AI tools can provide dashboards, risk scores, and visual reports that clients can understand and monitor in real time, strengthening trust and accountability in the lawyer-client relationship.

Driver 3: Competitive Pressures Among Firms

The legal sector is intensely competitive. Global firms compete not only with each other but also with boutique firms, in-house legal departments, and alternative legal service providers (ALSPs). Those who adopt AI can deliver higher-quality services faster, at lower cost, and with deeper insights.

For example, a firm using predictive analytics can give a client probabilistic forecasts of case outcomes, positioning itself as both innovative and strategically valuable. Meanwhile, firms that resist adopting AI risk losing market share, talent, and clients to those that embrace it.

AI adoption, therefore, is not just about internal efficiency—it is about maintaining relevance in a rapidly shifting marketplace.

Driver 4: Regulatory and Compliance Complexity

Modern businesses face growing regulatory scrutiny, from anti-money laundering (AML) obligations to data protection frameworks like GDPR and CCPA. Laws are updated constantly, often with overlapping or conflicting provisions across jurisdictions.

AI assists compliance teams by **monitoring legal updates in real time**, flagging potential risks, and automating reporting obligations. In industries such as banking or healthcare, where non-compliance can lead to massive fines and reputational damage, AI tools are becoming indispensable.

The legal profession, positioned as the guardian of compliance, must adopt the same technologies its clients rely on to manage regulatory exposure.

Driver 5: Access to Justice and Legal Innovation

Beyond corporate law, another driver is societal: access to justice. Millions of individuals cannot afford traditional legal services. AI-driven legal chatbots, document generators, and virtual assistants are bridging this gap by offering low-cost, accessible legal guidance.

For instance, platforms now help tenants contest unlawful evictions or assist individuals in drafting simple legal documents without the expense of a lawyer. While these tools cannot replace full legal representation, they reduce barriers and expand access to justice—an increasingly important mandate for modern legal systems.

Key Takeaway

The adoption of AI in legal practice is not a passing trend—it is the product of structural forces reshaping the profession. The explosion of legal data, heightened client expectations, competitive pressures, regulatory complexity, and the need for broader access to justice all converge on a single reality: AI is no longer optional. It is becoming a defining feature of how law is practiced, delivered, and experienced.

Lawyers who recognize these drivers will be better positioned to adapt, while those who resist risk being left behind in a profession where technological fluency is quickly becoming as important as legal expertise.

Myths vs. Realities: What AI Can and Cannot Do in Law

As AI continues to spread through the legal field, it has sparked both excitement and anxiety. Some believe that AI will soon replace lawyers entirely, while others dismiss it as little more than a gimmick. Both extremes misrepresent reality. AI is powerful, but it has limits. To understand its role in law, we must separate myths from practical truths.

Myth 1: AI Will Replace Lawyers Entirely

This is perhaps the most common fear. Movies and media often imagine AI "robot lawyers" arguing in court or replacing entire firms. The reality is different. AI excels at **narrow, well-defined tasks** such as scanning documents, identifying patterns, and summarizing text. It does not possess the creativity, empathy, or nuanced judgment required for advocacy, negotiation, or courtroom presence.

For instance, while an AI tool can flag unusual clauses in a contract, only a lawyer can evaluate whether accepting or rejecting that clause aligns with a client's business strategy or ethical considerations. In other words, AI supports legal decision-making but does not substitute the professional responsibility of lawyers.

Myth 2: AI Is Always Objective and Neutral

Another misconception is that AI delivers perfectly unbiased results. In reality, AI is only as objective as the data it is trained on. If past judicial decisions reflect systemic biases, predictive models built on those decisions may reproduce those same inequities.

A study in the U.S. highlighted how some risk-assessment tools used in criminal justice disproportionately flagged minority defendants as high-risk, even when controlling for other factors. This serves as a warning: AI must be audited, monitored, and applied responsibly to avoid reinforcing unfairness in the legal system.

Myth 3: AI Understands the Law Like a Lawyer

AI does not "understand" the law in the human sense. It processes language, identifies correlations, and applies statistical models. It does not grasp concepts such as justice, fairness, or context unless explicitly trained to recognize patterns associated with those terms.

For example, an AI system might predict the likely outcome of a case based on past rulings, but it cannot weigh moral considerations or account for unprecedented social shifts. That level of interpretation remains firmly in the domain of human lawyers and judges.

Myth 4: AI Is Too Expensive for Most Firms

At first, many assumed AI tools would be exclusive to global firms with massive technology budgets. But the market is rapidly changing. Cloud-based solutions, subscription models, and competitive pricing now make AI accessible to mid-sized and even small firms.

In fact, for smaller practices, AI can be a force multiplier—allowing them to compete with larger firms by automating tasks that would otherwise require more staff. Just as digital research tools eventually became standard across firms of all sizes, AI tools are moving in the same direction.

Reality: AI as a Partner, Not a Replacement

The truth lies between hype and skepticism. AI is neither a panacea nor a threat to the survival of the legal profession. It is best understood as a **partner**—a system that handles repetitive, data-heavy tasks so that lawyers can focus on strategy, interpretation, and advocacy.

AI can:

- Process millions of documents quickly and accurately.
- Identify patterns in judicial behavior and case law.
- Provide insights into risks, obligations, and compliance requirements.
- Support access to justice by offering affordable, basic guidance.

But AI cannot:

- Exercise independent moral or ethical judgment.
- Replace the human-to-human trust essential in attorney-client relationships.
- Argue persuasively in court or negotiate with empathy.
- Fully guarantee fairness or neutrality without human oversight.

Key Takeaway

The myths around AI in law often stem from overestimating or underestimating its capabilities. AI is not here to erase the role of lawyers—it is here to enhance it. By automating the routine, AI frees legal professionals to focus on higher-value work: advising clients, shaping strategy, and upholding justice.

The challenge ahead is not whether AI will dominate law, but how lawyers will integrate it responsibly, ensuring that efficiency does not come at the expense of fairness, ethics, or human judgment.

CHAPTER 2

Core AI Technologies in Law

Natural Language Processing (NLP) for Legal Text Analysis

The legal profession is built on language. Statutes, contracts, pleadings, and judgments are not just words on a page—they are binding instruments that shape rights, obligations, and outcomes. Yet the sheer volume and complexity of legal language present challenges even for the most skilled professionals. This is where **Natural Language Processing (NLP)**, a branch of artificial intelligence focused on teaching machines to read, interpret, and generate human language, plays a transformative role.

Why Legal Language Is Uniquely Challenging

Unlike everyday language, legal texts are characterized by dense syntax, technical terminology, and contextual ambiguity. A single clause can hinge on the placement of a comma, and the same term may carry different meanings in different jurisdictions or contexts.

For example, the word "consideration" in common law contracts does not mean thoughtfulness—it refers to the exchange of value required for an agreement to be enforceable. Similarly, statutes often contain cross-references and exceptions that require careful navigation.

Traditional keyword searches often fail in this environment. Searching for "consideration" in a database may retrieve irrelevant results unless the system understands its legal sense. NLP is designed to bridge this gap by teaching machines to recognize not only words but also the relationships and meanings behind them.

Core Applications of NLP in Law

1. **Legal Research and Case Law Analysis**
   NLP-powered search engines can go beyond keyword matching. They use semantic understanding to surface cases that address similar legal principles, even when different language is used. For instance, a query on "duty of care in negligence" might return cases phrased in terms of "standard of care" or "reasonable precautions."
2. **Contract Review and Analysis**
   NLP algorithms can scan thousands of contracts, identifying clauses related to risk, compliance, or unusual deviations. Instead of line-by-line manual review, lawyers receive flagged sections that require human judgment.
3. **Summarization of Legal Texts**
   NLP systems can generate concise summaries of lengthy judgments or regulatory documents, allowing lawyers to grasp the essentials quickly without losing critical details.
4. **Entity Recognition and Data Extraction**
   NLP tools can identify key parties, dates, obligations, and monetary amounts within contracts or litigation documents. This structured data can then feed into risk assessments or compliance systems.

Real-World Example: E-Discovery

In litigation, discovery often involves millions of emails, memos, and documents. NLP enhances **technology-assisted review (TAR)** by identifying relevant themes, spotting privileged communications, and clustering documents by topic. For example, in an antitrust case, NLP might surface communications involving "pricing strategy" even if that exact phrase was never used—because the system recognizes synonymous expressions.

This dramatically reduces the burden on legal teams and lowers costs, while improving accuracy compared to purely manual review.

Opportunities and Limitations

The opportunities of NLP in law are clear: faster research, more accurate contract review, and scalable document management. But NLP also has limitations. Context remains critical. Machines may misinterpret sarcasm, irony, or implicit meaning in witness statements or emails. Likewise, nuanced legal reasoning often requires cultural, historical, or ethical understanding that AI lacks.

Therefore, the most effective use of NLP is **augmented intelligence**—where algorithms perform the heavy lifting of processing and filtering, while lawyers apply expertise to interpret and act on the results.

Key Takeaway

Natural Language Processing is redefining how lawyers engage with legal texts. By enabling machines to read and interpret complex documents, NLP reduces time spent on repetitive tasks and enhances accuracy in research, review, and discovery. Yet its greatest value lies in partnership with human expertise. Lawyers who learn to work with NLP tools will not only save time but also unlock deeper insights, positioning themselves at the forefront of a profession where mastery of language—and now, machine language—is the key to success.

Machine Learning for Contract Review and Prediction Models

Contracts are the backbone of modern commerce. Every business deal, partnership, and transaction is framed by carefully drafted agreements. Yet contracts are also complex, lengthy, and often riddled with risks that are not immediately obvious. Traditionally, contract review demanded painstaking hours from junior associates and in-house legal teams. Now, **machine learning (ML)** is transforming this process by automating routine review and offering predictive insights that were once beyond human capacity.

Why Contract Review Is Ripe for Automation

A typical commercial contract might run dozens of pages, filled with boilerplate clauses alongside unique provisions. Reviewing just one agreement requires attention to details such as governing law, liability limits, termination rights, and compliance obligations. Multiply this by hundreds of contracts in a corporate portfolio, and the task becomes overwhelming.

Human reviewers often face fatigue, inconsistency, or oversight. Machine learning, by contrast, thrives on scale and pattern recognition. Once trained, an ML model can process thousands of contracts in minutes, flagging risks, identifying missing clauses, and surfacing unusual terms with remarkable consistency.

How Machine Learning Works in Contract Review

At its core, machine learning involves training algorithms on large datasets of legal documents. The system learns to recognize patterns—what a "standard indemnity clause" looks like, how "force majeure" provisions are typically worded, or what language signals high risk.

1. **Clause Detection and Classification**
   ML models categorize contract clauses into types (confidentiality, arbitration, liability, etc.), enabling quick navigation.
2. **Risk Flagging**
   Algorithms highlight clauses that deviate from market

norms—for example, unusually broad indemnity obligations or missing data privacy provisions.

3. **Compliance Checks**
   ML systems can check contracts against specific regulatory frameworks, flagging potential violations of GDPR, HIPAA, or industry-specific rules.

4. **Portfolio Insights**
   When applied across thousands of contracts, ML can reveal systemic risks, such as recurring unfavorable terms with vendors or widespread gaps in compliance.

Prediction Models in Law

Beyond review, machine learning powers **prediction models**— systems that forecast the likelihood of outcomes based on past data. In litigation, prediction models might estimate the probability of winning a motion or the expected damages in a specific type of case. In contracts, they can forecast negotiation dynamics or assess the likelihood of disputes arising from certain terms.

For example, if historical data shows that arbitration clauses with narrowly defined procedures reduce dispute costs by 40%, ML systems can flag the absence of such clauses as a risk factor. This allows lawyers not only to react to problems but to proactively shape better agreements.

Real-World Example: Corporate Mergers and Acquisitions

During mergers, due diligence often requires reviewing hundreds or even thousands of contracts across subsidiaries. Traditionally, this process took weeks, with large teams combing through documents manually.

Today, ML-powered tools can rapidly categorize contracts, extract key obligations (like change-of-control clauses), and highlight unusual provisions that may affect valuation or regulatory approval. This speeds up the transaction while improving accuracy—giving dealmakers greater confidence in their decisions.

Opportunities and Limitations

Machine learning offers immense efficiency and insight, but it is not flawless. Poorly trained models may misclassify clauses or overlook subtle risks. Prediction models are only as reliable as the data fed into them; if historical data is biased or incomplete, forecasts may mislead.

Moreover, contracts are not purely technical—they often reflect the unique business context, strategy, and risk tolerance of a client. Machine learning cannot replace the nuanced judgment of a lawyer who understands not only what is written in a clause but why it matters in practice.

Key Takeaway

Machine learning is revolutionizing contract review and prediction in law. It excels at processing vast volumes of agreements, spotting risks, and offering data-driven forecasts that enhance decision-making. Yet its true power emerges when combined with human expertise—where algorithms provide speed and consistency, and lawyers provide judgment and strategy. Together, they transform contract work from a reactive chore into a proactive, strategic advantage.

Generative AI for Drafting Documents and Summarization

Legal practice is built on documents: contracts, pleadings, opinions, memoranda, and regulatory filings. Drafting them is essential but time-intensive, often requiring repetitive language that varies only slightly between matters. This is where **generative AI**—AI systems capable of producing original text based on learned patterns—has become a game-changer. By automating parts of drafting and summarization, generative AI allows lawyers to shift their focus from routine writing to strategic thinking.

How Generative AI Works in Law

Generative AI models are trained on vast amounts of text data, enabling them to recognize linguistic patterns and produce human-like writing. In legal practice, these models can be fine-tuned on case law, contracts, or firm-specific templates to ensure relevance and accuracy.

Applications include:

- **Drafting First Versions**: AI can generate initial drafts of contracts, non-disclosure agreements, or compliance checklists, which lawyers then refine.
- **Summarization**: AI can condense lengthy judgments, statutes, or regulatory guidance into concise, structured summaries.
- **Customization**: Generative models can adapt templates to specific jurisdictions, industries, or client needs with minimal human input.

Drafting as Collaboration, Not Replacement

Generative AI does not replace the lawyer's role in drafting—it accelerates it. For example, if a lawyer needs to create a non-disclosure agreement (NDA), AI can instantly generate a draft based on standard clauses. The lawyer then adjusts the document to account for context, negotiation strategy, and client preferences.

This collaborative approach means lawyers spend less time reinventing standard documents and more time focusing on unique, value-adding provisions.

Summarization in Practice

Lawyers often face 100-page judgments or dense regulatory updates that must be understood quickly. Generative AI tools can create concise summaries highlighting key arguments, holdings, and implications.

For example, instead of reading an entire case, a lawyer might receive a summary that outlines:

- The legal issue addressed
- The court's reasoning
- The outcome
- Relevant citations to precedent

This allows for rapid orientation without sacrificing accuracy, though lawyers must always verify details before relying on AI-generated summaries.

Real-World Example: Regulatory Compliance Updates

Financial institutions often face constant changes in global regulations. Generative AI can scan new regulatory publications, summarize the key requirements, and flag areas of impact for the institution. Instead of compliance officers spending days parsing new rules, they receive clear, actionable overviews in minutes.

This not only saves time but also reduces the risk of missing critical updates in a rapidly evolving regulatory environment.

Opportunities and Risks

Generative AI provides unprecedented efficiency, but it comes with risks:

- **Hallucinations**: AI models sometimes produce inaccurate or fabricated information that looks plausible.
- **Overreliance**: Lawyers must resist the temptation to trust AI outputs without verification.
- **Confidentiality**: Inputting sensitive client data into generative platforms may risk breaches if not properly secured.

These limitations underline the importance of human oversight. Generative AI is a powerful drafting assistant, but it is not a substitute for legal expertise or ethical responsibility.

Key Takeaway

Generative AI has brought a new dimension to legal work by automating first drafts and creating concise, accurate summaries. Its value lies in accelerating routine processes, freeing lawyers to focus on judgment, creativity, and advocacy. The firms and professionals who learn to use generative AI responsibly will not only save time but also elevate the quality and accessibility of their legal services.

Legal Chatbots and Virtual Assistants in Client Services

The first interaction a client has with a law firm often determines the quality of the relationship. In the past, this meant scheduling calls, waiting for responses, or filling out intake forms manually. Today, **legal chatbots and virtual assistants** are redefining client service by providing immediate, accessible, and cost-effective interactions. These tools are not science fiction—they are already helping firms streamline intake, answer basic legal questions, and guide clients through complex processes.

What Legal Chatbots Can Do

Legal chatbots are AI-driven conversational tools that simulate human dialogue. They can:

- **Client Intake**: Gather initial information about a client's case, such as names, dates, and key facts.
- **FAQ Responses**: Answer common client questions about procedures, timelines, or documentation.
- **Document Generation**: Guide users through questionnaires and automatically draft standard documents like wills, NDAs, or employment agreements.
- **Case Updates**: Provide clients with real-time updates on case status without requiring staff intervention.

For instance, a family law firm might deploy a chatbot to help potential clients understand the steps involved in filing for divorce, including required forms and timelines. This empowers clients with information before they even speak with a lawyer.

Virtual Assistants for Lawyers and Clients

Beyond client-facing chatbots, virtual assistants also support lawyers internally. They can schedule meetings, retrieve case law, generate quick summaries of client files, or flag important deadlines. For busy practitioners, these assistants act like intelligent clerks, reducing administrative overhead and allowing more focus on substantive legal work.

Some platforms integrate both client-facing and internal functions. A corporate legal department, for example, might use a virtual assistant to triage service requests from business units, answer compliance queries, and escalate complex issues to human counsel when necessary.

Real-World Examples

1. **DoNotPay** – Often called the "robot lawyer," this chatbot helps users contest parking tickets, cancel subscriptions, and navigate small claims filings.
2. **Banking Sector Legal Bots** – Major banks deploy AI assistants to handle compliance inquiries, instantly answering whether a proposed transaction violates internal or regulatory rules.
3. **Law Firm Client Portals** – Firms increasingly integrate chatbots into portals, where clients can check case progress, upload documents, and receive notifications—all without waiting for email responses.

These examples illustrate that chatbots are not about replacing lawyers—they're about extending accessibility and efficiency.

Benefits and Challenges

Benefits:

- **Accessibility**: Clients can access legal guidance 24/7.
- **Efficiency**: Lawyers spend less time on repetitive inquiries.
- **Cost Reduction**: Automation lowers the cost of delivering routine services.
- **Client Satisfaction**: Faster responses build trust and engagement.

Challenges:

- **Accuracy**: Chatbots must be carefully programmed to avoid giving incorrect or misleading advice.
- **Scope of Service**: Ethical guidelines restrict bots from crossing into unauthorized practice of law.
- **Privacy Concerns**: Collecting sensitive client information requires robust data security measures.

The Future of AI-Enhanced Client Service

As NLP and generative AI improve, chatbots will become more conversational and context-aware. Future systems may integrate with court databases, track deadlines automatically, and even simulate negotiation scenarios. However, their role will remain supportive: handling routine tasks while lawyers deliver nuanced judgment, advocacy, and strategy.

Key Takeaway

Legal chatbots and virtual assistants represent a new frontier in client service. By automating intake, FAQs, and routine document generation, they reduce barriers to legal access while freeing lawyers to focus on higher-value work. The firms that adopt these tools responsibly will not only enhance efficiency but also strengthen relationships with clients in an era where responsiveness and accessibility are as important as legal expertise.

CHAPTER 3

AI in Legal Research

Automated Case Law and Statute Analysis

Legal research has always been the foundation of effective legal practice. A strong case depends not only on persuasive argument but on identifying the right precedents, statutes, and regulations to support it. Traditionally, this required exhaustive reading of casebooks, journals, and statutes—a laborious process prone to human error. With the rise of AI, however, **automated case law and statute analysis** has become a powerful tool, reshaping how lawyers prepare arguments and advise clients.

The Traditional Research Bottleneck

For decades, lawyers relied on digital databases like LexisNexis and Westlaw. While these tools were revolutionary in their time, they still required extensive manual effort. Lawyers had to design effective search queries, sift through thousands of results, and interpret which cases were relevant.

Even experienced researchers risked overlooking precedents, particularly when cases used different terminology to describe similar principles. For example, one ruling might use "duty of care" while another describes the same concept as "standard of care." These variations made comprehensive research slow and costly.

How AI Transforms Case and Statute Analysis

AI-powered legal research platforms go beyond keyword matching to understand the **meaning and context** of legal texts. Using natural language processing (NLP) and machine learning, these tools can:

1. **Interpret Queries in Plain Language**
   Lawyers can ask research questions in natural phrasing—e.g.,

"What cases discuss landlord liability for unsafe premises?"—and AI retrieves highly relevant cases, even if they don't use the exact same wording.

2. **Identify Key Holdings and Reasoning**
Instead of returning lengthy documents, AI tools highlight the core legal issue, the court's reasoning, and the outcome—saving lawyers hours of reading.

3. **Cross-Reference Statutes and Cases**
AI systems automatically link cases to the statutes they interpret, and vice versa, creating a dynamic map of legal authority.

4. **Spot Trends and Patterns**
By analyzing large bodies of case law, AI can show how courts in different jurisdictions treat similar issues, or how interpretations of a statute have shifted over time.

Real-World Example: Judicial Trend Analysis

In employment law, for instance, AI systems can track how courts apply "wrongful termination" standards across states. If one jurisdiction has increasingly narrowed the scope of what qualifies as wrongful termination, AI platforms can surface this trend, allowing lawyers to anticipate how future cases might be decided.

Similarly, in statutory interpretation, AI tools can reveal whether courts have consistently applied a particular tax exemption broadly or narrowly, helping lawyers craft arguments aligned with judicial tendencies.

Benefits of Automated Legal Research

- **Efficiency**: What once took days can now take minutes.
- **Accuracy**: AI reduces the risk of missing relevant authorities by expanding beyond exact wording.

- **Strategic Insight**: Lawyers gain not just cases but also a deeper understanding of how laws evolve and how judges apply them.
- **Accessibility**: Solo practitioners and smaller firms now have access to research power once limited to large firms with dedicated research teams.

Limitations and Risks

Despite its advantages, AI research tools are not infallible. Algorithms may misinterpret context, especially in niche areas of law. Statutory nuances—like exceptions buried in footnotes—still require human scrutiny. Furthermore, reliance on AI summaries may lead lawyers to overlook subtle but crucial details buried in the full text of an opinion.

Ethically, lawyers remain responsible for ensuring the accuracy of the authorities they cite. Courts have already sanctioned attorneys for submitting briefs that relied on AI-generated citations without verification. The lesson is clear: AI is a research partner, not a substitute for diligence.

Key Takeaway

Automated case law and statute analysis represents a quantum leap in legal research. By using AI to understand context, identify key holdings, and map legal authority, lawyers can conduct faster and more accurate research than ever before. Yet the role of human judgment remains central—AI may highlight the path, but lawyers must still walk it with careful interpretation and ethical responsibility.

Semantic Search vs. Keyword Search in Legal Databases

For decades, keyword search was the default method of legal research. Lawyers typed terms into a database and hoped that the right case or statute would appear in the results. While effective to a degree, keyword search has always struggled with the unique complexity of legal language. **Semantic search**, powered by AI, is now changing that paradigm—allowing legal professionals to find not just documents that match their words, but those that match their intent.

The Limits of Keyword Search

Keyword search works by matching the exact terms entered by the user to words in a database. While straightforward, this method has several limitations in the legal context:

- **Vocabulary Variations**: Courts may use different words to describe the same legal principle. A search for "duty of care" may miss cases phrased in terms of "standard of care."
- **Overinclusiveness**: A keyword search for "consideration" might return thousands of irrelevant results, including cases about "taking into consideration," rather than contract law.
- **Context Blindness**: Keyword search does not understand the meaning or importance of a term in its legal context.

The result is often information overload—long lists of documents that may contain the right answer buried among irrelevant results. Lawyers then spend hours sifting through noise to find substance.

The Rise of Semantic Search

Semantic search uses **natural language processing (NLP)** and **machine learning** to interpret the meaning of queries rather than just matching words. Instead of looking for exact text, it evaluates the **concepts and relationships** behind the language.

For example:

- A query for "landlord liability for unsafe premises" might surface cases involving "habitability," "premises defects," or "tenant safety," even if those words differ from the search terms.
- Searching "termination without cause employment contracts" could yield cases framed in terms of "at-will employment" or "wrongful dismissal."

Semantic search mimics how a skilled legal researcher thinks— understanding that different phrases can describe the same legal issue.

Advantages of Semantic Search

1. **Comprehensiveness** – Captures relevant cases that keyword search might miss due to vocabulary differences.
2. **Precision** – Filters out irrelevant documents by focusing on meaning rather than surface text.
3. **Accessibility** – Allows lawyers to phrase queries in natural language, lowering the barrier to effective research.
4. **Contextual Awareness** – Recognizes when terms are used in legal senses versus everyday usage.

In effect, semantic search brings lawyers closer to the information they need without requiring them to be experts in search syntax.

Real-World Impact

Legal research platforms like **Casetext's CARA A.I.** or **ROSS Intelligence** have demonstrated the power of semantic search. Instead of manually entering complex Boolean queries, a lawyer can upload a draft brief and the AI will suggest relevant authorities based on semantic similarity to the arguments presented.

This not only saves time but also reduces the risk of missing crucial precedents—an oversight that could weaken a case in court.

The Ongoing Role of Keyword Search

Despite its limitations, keyword search still has value. When lawyers know the exact term, statute number, or citation they are looking for, keyword search remains the fastest tool. For highly specific queries, it is often more efficient than semantic methods.

The future of legal research, therefore, is not a replacement of keyword search, but a **hybrid model** where keyword precision and semantic understanding complement each other.

Key Takeaway

The shift from keyword to semantic search marks a turning point in legal research. By focusing on meaning instead of mere words, semantic search tools reduce information overload and uncover precedents that might otherwise be missed. Lawyers who master both approaches—knowing when to use keyword exactness and when to leverage semantic depth—will gain a decisive advantage in the increasingly data-rich world of legal practice.

Using AI for Precedent Prediction and Case Relevance Ranking

Legal arguments are only as strong as the precedents supporting them. For centuries, lawyers have pored over case law to find decisions that align with their client's position and predict how courts might rule in the future. Traditionally, this has been a manual, time-consuming, and uncertain process. With AI, however, the landscape is changing. Modern systems now **predict precedent relevance** and **rank cases by their likelihood of influencing a decision**, giving lawyers a sharper and more strategic edge.

The Challenge of Precedent Research

The principle of *stare decisis*—that courts should follow established precedent—anchors legal reasoning. But in practice, applying it is far from straightforward. Thousands of new rulings are issued every year, often with subtle differences in fact patterns, jurisdiction, and judicial interpretation.

For example, two courts may both address negligence but emphasize different aspects of duty, causation, or damages. The challenge for lawyers is not just finding a precedent but finding the **most relevant precedent** for the specific facts and jurisdiction of their case.

How AI Predicts Precedent Relevance

AI-powered research platforms leverage **machine learning, natural language processing, and citation analysis** to assess which cases are most likely to matter. They do this by:

1. **Contextual Matching** – Comparing the facts and legal issues of a current case with past rulings to find close analogs, even if phrased differently.
2. **Citation Networks** – Mapping how often and in what context cases have been cited, revealing which precedents carry greater judicial weight.
3. **Fact Pattern Analysis** – Identifying similarities in parties, industries, or circumstances across cases to predict relevance.
4. **Outcome Forecasting** – Using historical data to estimate how likely a precedent is to be applied in a specific court or by a specific judge.

Case Relevance Ranking in Practice

Instead of presenting lawyers with hundreds of search results, AI systems now **rank cases by relevance and influence**. A negligence case, for instance, may be surfaced at the top of results not just because it contains matching terms, but because:

- It has been frequently cited in similar disputes.
- The reasoning closely aligns with the issues at hand.
- Courts in the same jurisdiction have relied on it in recent years.

This relevance ranking mirrors the strategic thinking of experienced lawyers, helping even junior associates quickly identify the strongest authorities.

Real-World Example: Judicial Behavior Insights

Platforms such as **Lex Machina** and **Ravel Law** have pioneered predictive precedent analysis. For example, they can reveal that Judge X tends to favor employer defenses in discrimination cases, or that a particular appellate court frequently narrows the scope of liability in tort claims.

Armed with this knowledge, lawyers can tailor their arguments, anticipate counterarguments, and advise clients more accurately on likely outcomes.

Opportunities and Risks

Opportunities:

- Streamlines the research process.
- Improves accuracy in identifying controlling precedent.
- Levels the playing field by giving smaller firms access to advanced insights.

Risks:

- Overreliance on algorithms may cause lawyers to miss novel arguments not reflected in past data.
- Prediction models can inherit biases from historical rulings, reinforcing existing inequities.
- Ethical risks arise if lawyers cite cases suggested by AI without independently verifying their authority and applicability.

Key Takeaway

AI-powered precedent prediction and case relevance ranking represent a major leap forward in legal research. By combining contextual understanding, citation analysis, and predictive modeling, these tools help lawyers identify the most persuasive authorities with speed and precision. Still, technology cannot replace legal judgment—only human lawyers can weigh whether a precedent is not just relevant but strategically compelling in advancing a client's case.

Enhancing Due Diligence with AI-Powered Data Mining

Due diligence is one of the most resource-intensive processes in legal practice. Whether for mergers and acquisitions, compliance audits, or litigation preparation, it involves reviewing massive volumes of documents—contracts, corporate filings, financial records, emails, and regulatory reports. Traditionally, teams of junior lawyers or paralegals spent weeks combing through data to identify risks. Today, **AI-powered data mining** is transforming due diligence by automating the extraction, classification, and risk analysis of vast datasets.

The Traditional Burden of Due Diligence

Consider a corporate acquisition. A buyer's legal team must assess thousands of contracts across subsidiaries to identify change-of-control provisions, liabilities, or compliance issues. Each document might contain subtle variations that could affect deal value. Missing just one high-risk clause could have multimillion-dollar consequences.

This level of review is time-consuming, error-prone, and expensive. It also limits the scope of due diligence—lawyers often focus only on the most critical documents, leaving other risks hidden.

How AI-Powered Data Mining Works

AI data mining combines **natural language processing (NLP), machine learning, and pattern recognition** to rapidly process unstructured legal data. These systems can:

1. **Classify Documents** – Automatically sort contracts, filings, or correspondence into relevant categories (leases, employment contracts, vendor agreements, etc.).
2. **Extract Key Terms** – Identify parties, dates, monetary values, obligations, and unusual clauses.
3. **Spot Risks** – Flag deviations from standard terms, such as unlimited liability, missing termination clauses, or non-compliance with regulations.
4. **Summarize Findings** – Generate structured reports highlighting critical issues for lawyer review.

This automation allows legal teams to scale due diligence efforts without proportional increases in manpower or cost.

Real-World Example: Mergers and Acquisitions

In a high-value merger, AI tools can review thousands of contracts in a fraction of the time it would take human reviewers. For instance, the system might highlight that 20% of vendor contracts contain restrictive exclusivity clauses, or that key employment agreements lack enforceable non-compete provisions.

By surfacing these issues early, lawyers can advise clients on renegotiation, valuation adjustments, or even deal restructuring—decisions that directly impact the success of the transaction.

Beyond Transactions: Compliance and Litigation

Due diligence is not limited to M&A. AI-powered data mining also enhances:

- **Regulatory Compliance**: Companies can monitor ongoing contractual and reporting obligations across jurisdictions.
- **Litigation Readiness**: AI systems can mine internal data to identify potential liabilities before a dispute escalates.
- **Fraud Detection**: Algorithms can detect unusual financial or contractual patterns that suggest misconduct.

These applications extend the value of AI beyond single transactions into continuous risk management.

Opportunities and Limitations

Opportunities:

- Dramatically reduces review time and cost.
- Expands the scope of due diligence beyond what is humanly feasible.
- Increases accuracy by catching details that may be overlooked.

Limitations:

- AI may misinterpret context, such as industry-specific terms or jurisdictional nuances.
- Overreliance on automation risks overlooking strategic considerations not captured in text (e.g., reputational risks).
- Data security is paramount—feeding sensitive documents into AI systems requires strict safeguards.

Key Takeaway

AI-powered data mining is revolutionizing due diligence, turning a traditionally labor-intensive process into a strategic advantage. By automating document classification, risk identification, and reporting, AI enables lawyers to focus on high-level analysis and negotiation. Still, the human role remains essential—lawyers must interpret findings, assess context, and translate insights into actionable advice. Together, AI and human expertise elevate due diligence from a compliance exercise to a driver of smarter business decisions.

CHAPTER 4

Contract Analysis and Management

AI-Driven Contract Review and Redlining

Contracts are the DNA of business relationships. They define obligations, allocate risks, and establish remedies when things go wrong. Yet reviewing contracts has long been one of the most tedious and time-consuming tasks in legal practice. AI-driven tools are now changing this reality by automating contract review and **redlining**—the process of identifying, comparing, and suggesting edits to contract provisions. This technology not only accelerates legal work but also elevates the quality and consistency of contract negotiation.

The Traditional Pain Points of Contract Review

A typical review requires lawyers to examine every clause carefully—checking for risks, ensuring compliance, and comparing terms against market standards. In large transactions, this could mean reading hundreds of contracts in compressed timelines.

Common challenges include:

- **Volume**: Thousands of pages to review under strict deadlines.
- **Consistency**: Different reviewers may interpret clauses differently, leading to inconsistent feedback.
- **Fatigue**: Human error increases when reviewing repetitive documents.
- **Inefficiency**: Lawyers often spend hours reviewing boilerplate provisions that rarely change.

These pain points create delays, inflate costs, and increase the risk of overlooking critical issues.

How AI Enhances Contract Review

AI tools, powered by **natural language processing (NLP)** and **machine learning**, streamline review in several ways:

1. **Clause Identification** – Automatically detects clauses such as indemnification, termination, confidentiality, or force majeure.
2. **Risk Flagging** – Highlights provisions that deviate from market standards or organizational playbooks, such as unusually broad liability clauses.
3. **Compliance Checking** – Compares terms against regulatory requirements (e.g., GDPR, data retention laws).
4. **Version Comparison (Redlining)** – Automatically identifies differences between contract drafts, showing additions, deletions, and modifications.
5. **Playbook Integration** – Aligns contracts with firm- or client-specific negotiation guidelines, suggesting edits consistent with preferred positions.

Redlining with AI

Redlining is one of the most powerful applications of AI in contracts. Traditionally, lawyers manually compared drafts side by side, a process vulnerable to oversight. AI systems can now:

- Detect subtle changes in wording that shift risk allocation (e.g., "best efforts" vs. "reasonable efforts").
- Suggest alternative language aligned with standard negotiation strategies.
- Provide contextual explanations for why a change may be risky or favorable.

This transforms redlining from a manual proofreading exercise into a strategic tool for negotiation.

Real-World Example: Commercial Lease Review

Consider a retail company negotiating dozens of lease agreements across multiple locations. AI tools can quickly flag provisions where landlords attempt to shift maintenance obligations to tenants—highlighting these deviations across contracts in seconds. The legal team can then standardize responses, ensuring consistent negotiation positions across all deals.

Opportunities and Limitations

Opportunities:

- Speeds up contract review from days to hours.
- Improves accuracy and reduces missed risks.
- Standardizes negotiations across large portfolios.
- Frees lawyers to focus on high-value negotiation strategy.

Limitations:

- AI may misinterpret highly customized or novel provisions.
- Contextual business considerations (e.g., whether to accept risk for strategic reasons) still require human judgment.
- Overreliance may lead to missed nuances if lawyers fail to review AI outputs critically.

Key Takeaway

AI-driven contract review and redlining are transforming one of the most time-consuming aspects of legal practice. By automating clause detection, risk analysis, and version comparison, AI allows lawyers to move faster, negotiate smarter, and deliver more consistent results. But technology alone is not enough—the most effective outcomes arise when AI handles the repetitive groundwork and lawyers apply judgment, creativity, and client-specific strategy to the negotiation process.

Identifying Risks, Obligations, and Compliance Gaps

Every contract carries a story of rights, duties, and potential pitfalls. For businesses, the difference between success and costly disputes often lies in how well these risks and obligations are identified upfront. Traditionally, spotting risks required lawyers to comb through each line, hunting for hidden liabilities or missing protections. Now, **AI-powered tools** are enhancing this process—scanning contracts with speed and accuracy, surfacing issues that could otherwise remain buried until it's too late.

The Hidden Risks in Contracts

Contracts are designed to allocate responsibility, but vague or unfavorable terms can create traps for the unwary. Common risks include:

- **Unlimited liability clauses** that expose one party to disproportionate financial consequences.
- **Ambiguous termination provisions** that make it difficult to exit an unfavorable deal.
- **Inconsistent obligations** across different contracts in a portfolio, creating compliance conflicts.
- **Regulatory gaps** where terms fail to meet the standards of laws like GDPR, HIPAA, or local labor rules.

These risks are rarely obvious at first glance—especially in lengthy documents filled with boilerplate language.

How AI Flags Risks and Obligations

AI systems trained on thousands of contracts can recognize patterns and deviations far faster than humans. Their capabilities include:

1. **Obligation Extraction** – Identifying who must do what, by when, and under what conditions. For example, automatically flagging delivery deadlines or reporting requirements.
2. **Risk Detection** – Highlighting clauses that deviate from market norms, such as indemnity obligations that are unusually broad.
3. **Gap Analysis** – Comparing contracts against regulatory frameworks or internal playbooks to flag missing provisions (e.g., absent data protection clauses in vendor agreements).
4. **Portfolio-Level Risk Assessment** – Reviewing hundreds of contracts simultaneously to detect systemic risks, such as inconsistent dispute resolution provisions.

Real-World Example: Data Privacy Compliance

Consider a multinational corporation outsourcing IT services to multiple vendors. AI-powered review tools can scan each vendor contract to ensure compliance with data privacy regulations like GDPR. If one agreement lacks required breach notification timelines, the system flags it as a compliance gap. The legal team can then renegotiate or amend the agreement before regulatory penalties arise.

Benefits of AI in Risk Identification

- **Efficiency**: Detects risks across thousands of contracts in hours rather than weeks.

- **Consistency**: Applies uniform standards, avoiding discrepancies between different reviewers.
- **Strategic Insight**: Helps firms not only spot problems but also benchmark against industry norms.
- **Preventive Value**: Surfaces risks before they escalate into disputes, regulatory fines, or reputational damage.

Limitations and Human Oversight

AI cannot fully capture the **contextual dimension** of risk. For instance, an "unlimited liability" clause might be acceptable in a low-risk service contract but catastrophic in a high-risk supply chain agreement. Business strategy, client risk tolerance, and negotiation dynamics are factors only lawyers can evaluate.

Similarly, AI models are limited by their training data—novel contractual arrangements or industry-specific risks may escape detection. This makes human oversight indispensable.

Key Takeaway

AI is redefining how lawyers identify risks, obligations, and compliance gaps in contracts. By automating detection and analysis, it transforms contract review from a reactive process into a proactive safeguard. Yet, the final judgment remains with human lawyers, who must weigh not only what the contract says but what it means in practice. The partnership between AI efficiency and human expertise ensures contracts are not just legally sound, but strategically aligned with business goals.

Smart Contract Creation and Blockchain Integration

Contracts have always been about trust: one party promises to perform, and the other expects enforcement if things go wrong. Traditionally, that enforcement depended on human oversight— lawyers drafting terms, courts interpreting disputes, and regulators monitoring compliance. With the rise of **smart contracts** powered by **blockchain technology**, some of these functions are shifting from human institutions to automated systems. Smart contracts promise speed, transparency, and security, but they also raise new legal and ethical challenges.

What Are Smart Contracts?

A smart contract is a **self-executing agreement** written in computer code and stored on a blockchain. Instead of relying on manual enforcement, the terms of the contract are programmed so that obligations automatically trigger when conditions are met.

For example:

- In a supply chain contract, payment could be released automatically once goods are delivered and verified by a tracking system.
- In real estate, ownership of property could transfer instantly when funds are deposited into escrow via blockchain.

The appeal lies in automation—removing intermediaries and reducing delays, disputes, and administrative costs.

The Role of Blockchain

Blockchain provides the infrastructure for smart contracts. Because it is **decentralized and tamper-resistant**, blockchain ensures that once a contract is coded and executed, it cannot be altered without consensus. This enhances:

- **Trust**: Parties rely on code, not intermediaries, to enforce obligations.
- **Transparency**: All participants can view the transaction history.
- **Security**: Cryptographic protections reduce the risk of fraud or unauthorized changes.

These features make blockchain attractive in industries where trust deficits or high transaction costs have historically slowed commerce.

Applications in Legal Practice

1. **Financial Services** – Smart contracts can automate loan disbursements, repayments, and compliance with regulatory triggers.
2. **Intellectual Property** – Creators can use smart contracts to automate royalty payments when content is streamed or licensed.
3. **Supply Chains** – Complex chains of vendors and distributors can be managed with contracts that automatically enforce delivery milestones.
4. **Dispute Resolution** – Some blockchain platforms include built-in arbitration mechanisms to resolve conflicts without courts.

Opportunities and Challenges

Opportunities:

- **Efficiency**: Reduces administrative overhead and delays.
- **Accuracy**: Eliminates ambiguity by encoding precise, executable terms.
- **Global Transactions**: Simplifies cross-border agreements by bypassing traditional enforcement mechanisms.

Challenges:

- **Legal Ambiguity**: Many jurisdictions lack clear frameworks for recognizing smart contracts as legally binding.
- **Code vs. Context**: Contracts often require interpretation— what happens if circumstances change or an unforeseen event occurs?
- **Error Risks**: A coding mistake can lock parties into unintended obligations, with limited recourse once deployed.
- **Regulatory Compliance**: Automated enforcement may conflict with consumer protection or data privacy laws.

Real-World Example: Insurance Payouts

Some insurers now experiment with smart contracts for travel insurance. If a flight is canceled, blockchain systems automatically trigger payouts without requiring claims forms or manual review. While efficient, these systems raise questions: what if the cancellation occurs for a reason not covered under policy language? Should human discretion override the code?

This tension illustrates the balance between automation and interpretation—a balance central to the future of smart contracts.

Key Takeaway

Smart contracts and blockchain integration represent a bold shift in how agreements are created, executed, and enforced. They offer speed, transparency, and reliability, but also introduce risks where human judgment and flexibility are still essential. Lawyers must evolve from mere drafters of words to **architects of code and context**, ensuring that automation enhances—rather than undermines—the principles of fairness and justice at the heart of law.

Lifecycle Management: Drafting, Negotiation, Execution, Monitoring

Contracts are not static documents; they are **living instruments** that evolve from initial drafts to execution and ongoing performance. Managing the entire lifecycle—drafting, negotiation, execution, and monitoring—has historically been fragmented, with each stage handled in isolation. AI is now enabling a **unified, end-to-end approach** to contract lifecycle management (CLM), helping organizations gain efficiency, consistency, and control.

Drafting: From Templates to Intelligent Automation

Traditional drafting often began with copying templates or reusing past contracts. While efficient, this approach risked overlooking updates in law or organizational policies.

AI-powered drafting tools take this further by:

- Suggesting clauses based on contract type, industry standards, and jurisdiction.
- Adapting language dynamically to client-specific needs.

- Flagging outdated or non-compliant provisions before they make it into a draft.

This ensures consistency while reducing reliance on manual template updates.

Negotiation: Data-Driven Bargaining

Negotiation has always been part art, part science. AI now adds a data-driven dimension by:

- Highlighting "market standard" terms, giving lawyers leverage to push back against unreasonable demands.
- Analyzing prior negotiations to predict likely points of contention.
- Suggesting fallback clauses aligned with a company's playbook when compromises are needed.

For example, if a supplier insists on limiting liability, AI may recommend alternative caps based on patterns from past deals, providing negotiators with ready-made, acceptable counteroffers.

Execution: Streamlined and Secure

Executing contracts used to mean printing, signing, scanning, and storing paper copies. Today, e-signature platforms integrated with AI tools ensure:

- Faster turnaround times.
- Verification of signatories to reduce fraud.
- Automatic archiving and indexing for future retrieval.

Smart contracts on blockchain go one step further by executing obligations automatically once predefined conditions are met— removing friction from the execution stage entirely.

Monitoring: Turning Contracts Into Active Assets

The most overlooked stage of the lifecycle is **post-signature monitoring**. Many obligations—reporting deadlines, renewal dates, compliance triggers—occur months or years after execution. Without active tracking, businesses risk missed obligations, penalties, or disputes.

AI enhances monitoring by:

- Extracting key dates, obligations, and triggers from contracts.
- Sending automated reminders for deadlines or renewals.
- Alerting stakeholders to potential breaches or compliance issues.
- Aggregating data across portfolios to identify systemic risks or opportunities (e.g., renegotiating underused vendor agreements).

For example, an AI system might alert a company that 40% of its vendor contracts will automatically renew within 90 days unless terminated—giving the business time to renegotiate terms.

Opportunities and Challenges

Opportunities:

- Provides a single, integrated view of contracts across their lifecycle.
- Reduces inefficiencies and errors caused by siloed processes.

- Enables proactive management of obligations and risks.
- Turns contracts into sources of strategic insight, not just static records.

Challenges:

- Requires integration with existing business systems (finance, procurement, HR).
- Raises data security concerns given the sensitive nature of contracts.
- May still struggle with highly bespoke agreements that defy automation.

Key Takeaway

AI-powered lifecycle management transforms contracts from static documents into **dynamic, managed assets**. By streamlining drafting, negotiation, execution, and monitoring, it reduces risk, ensures compliance, and drives efficiency. Most importantly, it empowers lawyers and businesses to shift from reactive firefighting to proactive strategy—using contracts not just to document deals, but to drive growth and innovation.

CHAPTER 5

Litigation, Dispute Resolution, and Predictive Justice

AI for Case Outcome Prediction and Risk Assessment

Litigation is inherently uncertain. Even the most experienced lawyers cannot guarantee how a judge or jury will rule, how long a case will take, or what financial exposure a client might face. For decades, legal strategy relied on professional judgment, intuition, and precedent analysis. Today, **AI-powered outcome prediction and risk assessment tools** are introducing a new level of clarity—helping lawyers advise clients with greater confidence and precision.

The Traditional Challenge of Prediction

Lawyers have always assessed case prospects by studying precedent, analyzing fact patterns, and drawing on experience with specific courts or judges. While valuable, this method has limits:

- **Subjectivity**: Predictions vary depending on a lawyer's experience and biases.
- **Data Overload**: Courts produce far more decisions than any human can realistically track.
- **Uncertainty**: Even strong cases can falter due to procedural issues, judicial discretion, or unexpected evidence.

Clients, especially corporate ones, often want more than a "likely" or "probably"—they want data-driven estimates of success and financial exposure.

How AI Predicts Case Outcomes

AI systems trained on **historical case law, judicial behavior, and litigation data** can estimate the probability of outcomes in ways humans cannot. These systems analyze:

1. **Judicial History** – How a judge has ruled in similar cases, their tendencies on motions, and their average timelines.
2. **Fact Pattern Similarity** – Comparing the current case to thousands of past ones with overlapping issues and facts.
3. **Litigation Trends** – Evaluating how certain types of claims fare in specific courts or jurisdictions.
4. **Settlement Patterns** – Predicting likelihood of settlement and typical ranges of damages or settlements in comparable disputes.

For example, AI might estimate that a patent infringement claim filed in a certain federal district has a **65% chance of dismissal at summary judgment**—insight that helps clients decide whether to litigate, negotiate, or settle.

Risk Assessment Beyond Win or Lose

Outcome prediction is not just about victory or defeat—it is about **risk management**. AI tools generate models of potential scenarios, including:

- The range of possible damages.
- Likelihood of appeal.
- Expected litigation costs by stage.
- Probabilities of settlement versus trial.

This allows lawyers to present clients with **decision trees** and **probabilistic forecasts**, transforming vague conversations into quantifiable risk assessments.

Real-World Example: Corporate Litigation Strategy

A multinational facing a class-action lawsuit might use AI tools to evaluate:

- How often similar claims have succeeded in that jurisdiction.
- Which arguments have historically persuaded courts.
- The settlement amounts typically reached in comparable cases.

Armed with this data, executives can make informed decisions about whether to fight in court, pursue early settlement, or restructure operations to reduce future exposure.

Opportunities and Limitations

Opportunities:

- Enhances client trust through transparent, data-backed advice.
- Helps companies make cost-benefit decisions about litigation.
- Improves negotiation leverage by quantifying risks.
- Levels the playing field, giving smaller firms access to insights once reserved for those with vast resources.

Limitations:

- Predictions depend on historical data—AI may struggle with novel cases or emerging legal issues.
- Biases in past rulings can be reproduced in AI models.
- Human judgment remains essential for interpreting unique facts, witness credibility, or public policy considerations that no algorithm can fully capture.

Key Takeaway

AI-powered case outcome prediction and risk assessment mark a turning point in litigation strategy. By leveraging vast datasets and judicial analytics, these tools give lawyers and clients a clearer picture of legal risks and opportunities. Still, the future of litigation is not about surrendering strategy to machines—it is about blending human judgment with AI-driven insights to make smarter, more strategic decisions in an unpredictable legal environment.

Virtual Courtrooms and AI-Enhanced Legal Proceedings

For centuries, the courtroom has been a physical space: lawyers presenting arguments, judges presiding, witnesses testifying, and clerks recording proceedings. The COVID-19 pandemic accelerated a dramatic shift, pushing courts around the world to adopt **virtual hearings** and remote proceedings. Now, with AI integrated into these digital environments, the very architecture of justice is evolving. Virtual courtrooms are no longer just a necessity—they are becoming an opportunity to reimagine how legal proceedings can be conducted with greater accessibility, efficiency, and fairness.

The Rise of Virtual Courtrooms

Before the pandemic, only a handful of jurisdictions experimented with remote hearings, mostly for procedural matters. In 2020, entire justice systems had to pivot online, using platforms like Zoom, Microsoft Teams, or court-specific portals. This shift demonstrated that many hearings—status conferences, motions, even appellate arguments—could be conducted virtually without compromising core judicial functions.

The success of this experiment has inspired courts to retain virtual proceedings even as physical courthouses reopened. In many jurisdictions, hybrid models now allow parties to choose between in-person and remote appearances, depending on the case type and needs of participants.

How AI Enhances Virtual Proceedings

AI is adding new dimensions to virtual courts by automating and streamlining aspects of the judicial process:

1. **Transcription and Summarization** – AI generates real-time transcripts and concise summaries of hearings, ensuring accurate records and saving clerks hours of manual work.
2. **Language Translation** – Multilingual AI systems allow participants who speak different languages to follow proceedings in real time.
3. **Scheduling and Case Management** – AI tools help courts allocate resources, assign judges, and manage calendars more efficiently.
4. **Evidence Presentation** – AI-assisted platforms can automatically organize exhibits, highlight relevant sections, and ensure smooth digital presentation during hearings.
5. **Accessibility Tools** – Voice recognition and text-to-speech systems make proceedings more inclusive for participants with disabilities.

Real-World Example: AI in Remote Justice

In China, "smart courts" have integrated AI tools to manage case filings, provide legal guidance to litigants, and even recommend outcomes in simple disputes. In the U.S., courts in states like Michigan and Texas continue to conduct thousands of hearings virtually, with AI-assisted transcription ensuring accuracy and efficiency.

These examples show that AI in virtual courts is not futuristic—it is already happening, reshaping expectations of how justice can be delivered.

Opportunities and Challenges

Opportunities:

- **Access to Justice**: Virtual hearings reduce travel costs and logistical barriers, making courts more accessible to low-income litigants and those in rural areas.
- **Efficiency**: Automated scheduling and case management reduce backlogs.
- **Consistency**: AI transcription and summarization improve record accuracy.
- **Globalization**: AI translation tools enable cross-border legal proceedings in international disputes.

Challenges:

- **Digital Divide**: Not all litigants have reliable internet or technology access.
- **Fairness Concerns**: Remote hearings may disadvantage parties who lack technological literacy or strong connectivity.
- **Privacy and Security**: Virtual proceedings raise risks of unauthorized recording, data breaches, or cyberattacks.
- **Human Element**: Nonverbal cues and courtroom dynamics can be harder to assess through screens, affecting witness credibility evaluations.

Key Takeaway

Virtual courtrooms, enhanced by AI, represent a profound evolution in how justice is delivered. They expand access, reduce delays, and improve record-keeping while raising new questions about fairness, privacy, and inclusivity. The challenge for the legal profession is not whether virtual hearings will remain, but how to integrate AI responsibly—ensuring that efficiency never comes at the cost of justice.

Tools for E-Discovery and Evidence Management

Litigation today generates mountains of evidence—emails, text messages, financial records, social media posts, and more. In large cases, the volume of digital evidence can reach millions of files, making manual review virtually impossible. This is where **AI-powered e-discovery and evidence management tools** have transformed litigation, enabling lawyers to identify relevant material quickly, accurately, and cost-effectively.

The Challenge of Modern Evidence

Before AI, discovery often consumed the largest share of litigation costs. Teams of junior lawyers or paralegals manually reviewed documents for relevance, privilege, or confidentiality. This process was not only expensive but also error-prone, with critical evidence sometimes missed in the sheer volume of data.

The rise of electronic discovery (*e-discovery*) has amplified this challenge. A single corporate email server might hold terabytes of data—far more than humans can feasibly review in time-sensitive cases.

How AI Enhances E-Discovery

AI-powered tools, particularly those using **natural language processing (NLP)** and **machine learning**, automate much of the discovery process. Their capabilities include:

1. **Technology-Assisted Review (TAR)** – Algorithms learn from attorney-reviewed samples, then apply those patterns across massive datasets to prioritize relevant documents.
2. **Keyword Expansion** – AI identifies synonyms and related terms to ensure searches capture variations (e.g., "kickback" vs. "improper payment").
3. **Clustering and Topic Modeling** – Groups documents by themes, allowing lawyers to explore issues rather than comb through individual files.
4. **Privilege Detection** – Flags communications likely protected by attorney-client privilege, reducing the risk of inadvertent disclosure.
5. **Sentiment and Behavior Analysis** – Identifies unusual communication patterns that may signal misconduct (e.g., sudden drops in email volume before fraud events).

Evidence Management Beyond Discovery

AI also plays a role after documents are identified. Evidence must be **organized, stored, and presented** in ways courts can accept. AI systems can:

- Tag and index documents for rapid retrieval.
- Create timelines of key communications.
- Generate summaries of document sets for trial preparation.
- Assist in building visual exhibits for courtroom presentation.

This integration ensures that evidence is not only found but also meaningfully used.

Real-World Example: Corporate Fraud Investigation

In a multinational fraud case, investigators faced over five million documents, including multilingual emails. AI tools narrowed this to a manageable set by identifying suspicious clusters of communications related to unusual transactions. The system flagged coded language in emails that human reviewers might have dismissed as innocuous, ultimately leading to key evidence of collusion.

Opportunities and Risks

Opportunities:

- Reduces discovery costs dramatically.
- Improves accuracy by identifying hidden patterns humans might miss.
- Speeds up litigation, reducing court delays.
- Levels the playing field—small firms can handle massive datasets with the right tools.

Risks:

- AI models may miss context or misclassify sensitive documents.
- Overreliance can create ethical issues if lawyers fail to independently verify findings.
- Data privacy and cybersecurity are heightened concerns when vast troves of sensitive information are processed.

Key Takeaway

AI-powered e-discovery and evidence management tools are revolutionizing litigation. They make it possible to navigate the overwhelming volume of modern digital evidence while saving time and costs. Yet, the lawyer's role remains central: AI can find the documents, but only humans can interpret their meaning, connect them to legal strategy, and persuade courts of their significance.

AI in Alternative Dispute Resolution (ADR)

Not all conflicts end up in court. Businesses and individuals often turn to **alternative dispute resolution (ADR)**—including arbitration, mediation, and negotiation—to resolve matters more efficiently and privately. As with litigation, ADR is now being reshaped by artificial intelligence. From online dispute resolution platforms to AI-assisted mediators, technology is creating faster, more accessible ways to settle disputes while raising important questions about fairness and human judgment.

Why ADR Is Ripe for AI

ADR has long been favored for its **efficiency, flexibility, and confidentiality**. But traditional ADR can still be costly, time-consuming, and dependent on human availability. Disputes involving thousands of contracts, cross-border transactions, or consumer complaints generate workloads that overwhelm traditional processes.

AI is well-suited for ADR because it thrives in structured environments where disputes revolve around data, documents, and repetitive issues.

AI in Mediation and Arbitration

1. **Online Dispute Resolution (ODR) Platforms**
   AI-driven systems guide parties through structured
   negotiation processes. For example, e-commerce disputes
   (like refund claims) can often be resolved entirely online,
   with AI suggesting settlements based on similar cases.
2. **AI-Powered Mediation Support**
   Algorithms can analyze negotiation histories, highlight areas
   of agreement, and suggest compromise solutions. Instead of
   replacing mediators, AI provides tools that accelerate
   consensus-building.
3. **Arbitration Assistance**
   AI systems can manage case filings, schedule hearings, and
   even generate draft procedural orders. Some platforms
   experiment with AI-driven recommendations for awards in
   low-value disputes, subject to human arbitrator approval.

Real-World Example: E-Commerce and Consumer Disputes

Platforms like **eBay** and **Alibaba** have pioneered AI-assisted ODR
systems. When buyers and sellers disagree, AI reviews transaction
records, communication history, and market norms to suggest a fair
resolution. Most disputes are settled automatically, without human
arbitrators.

This model has inspired broader adoption: governments in Canada,
the UK, and the EU are piloting AI-driven ODR platforms for small
claims disputes, reducing court backlogs and giving citizens faster
access to justice.

Opportunities and Challenges

Opportunities:

- **Accessibility**: Makes dispute resolution affordable and available to individuals and small businesses.
- **Efficiency**: Reduces the time and cost of resolving routine disputes.
- **Consistency**: Offers standardized approaches to repetitive issues.
- **Scalability**: Handles thousands of disputes simultaneously—something human mediators and arbitrators cannot.

Challenges:

- **Fairness Concerns**: Algorithms may favor efficiency over nuance, risking outcomes that feel impersonal or unjust.
- **Transparency**: Parties may question how AI reaches its recommendations if systems lack explainability.
- **Human Element**: Some disputes—especially emotional or relationship-driven ones—require empathy and human understanding AI cannot replicate.
- **Legal Recognition**: Questions remain about whether AI-driven decisions will be enforceable in all jurisdictions.

Key Takeaway

AI in ADR is expanding access to justice by making dispute resolution faster, cheaper, and more scalable. From consumer complaints to cross-border commercial disputes, AI tools are becoming trusted partners in negotiation, mediation, and arbitration. Yet, technology cannot replace the human touch where trust, empathy, and nuanced judgment are essential. The future of ADR lies in **hybrid models**—where AI handles structure and scale, and human mediators or arbitrators ensure fairness and legitimacy.

CHAPTER 6

Compliance, Ethics, and Regulatory Applications

AI in Regulatory Monitoring and Compliance Audits

Modern businesses operate in an increasingly complex regulatory environment. From financial reporting to data privacy, from environmental standards to labor laws, organizations must comply with a web of overlapping rules that evolve constantly across jurisdictions. Failure to comply is not merely inconvenient—it can mean multimillion-dollar fines, reputational damage, or even criminal liability. Traditionally, legal teams and compliance officers relied on manual monitoring and periodic audits. Today, **AI-driven tools** are revolutionizing compliance by providing continuous monitoring, automated audits, and predictive insights.

The Rising Tide of Regulation

Globalization and digitization have multiplied compliance challenges:

- **Data Protection**: Regulations like the EU's GDPR or California's CCPA impose strict rules on how companies handle personal data.
- **Financial Oversight**: Banks must comply with anti-money laundering (AML) and "Know Your Customer" (KYC) requirements.
- **Environmental Rules**: Companies face new reporting obligations on emissions, waste, and sustainability practices.
- **Sector-Specific Laws**: Healthcare, pharmaceuticals, and defense industries face highly specialized regulatory frameworks.

Staying compliant means tracking thousands of legal changes across multiple jurisdictions—an impossible task for humans alone.

How AI Supports Regulatory Monitoring

AI systems leverage **natural language processing (NLP)** and **machine learning** to continuously scan and interpret regulatory changes worldwide. Their capabilities include:

1. **Regulatory Tracking** – Monitoring government websites, regulatory bulletins, and legal updates in real time.
2. **Change Alerts** – Flagging new obligations and comparing them against an organization's current policies.
3. **Risk Mapping** – Linking regulatory changes to affected contracts, operations, or business units.
4. **Predictive Insights** – Forecasting likely regulatory trends (e.g., stricter data privacy rules in emerging markets) based on global developments.

This turns compliance from a reactive exercise into a proactive strategy.

AI in Compliance Audits

Beyond monitoring, AI streamlines compliance audits by:

- **Automating Document Review**: Extracting relevant terms from policies, contracts, and reports to check for regulatory alignment.
- **Identifying Gaps**: Comparing company practices against legal requirements and industry benchmarks.
- **Continuous Auditing**: Enabling "always-on" compliance checks rather than periodic, resource-heavy reviews.
- **Reporting**: Generating audit-ready reports that regulators can verify, reducing preparation time.

For example, an AI tool could automatically review a company's vendor contracts to ensure each includes GDPR-mandated data processing clauses—flagging those that do not for legal follow-up.

Real-World Example: Banking Compliance

Large banks face enormous compliance challenges, with regulators imposing heavy fines for AML failures. AI-powered compliance platforms now analyze transactions in real time, identifying unusual patterns that suggest money laundering. Instead of reviewing thousands of alerts manually, compliance teams receive prioritized, high-risk cases for investigation.

This approach not only reduces regulatory risk but also improves efficiency—cutting compliance costs while strengthening enforcement.

Opportunities and Challenges

Opportunities:

- **Efficiency**: Automates tasks that once required armies of auditors.
- **Accuracy**: Reduces human error in tracking and interpreting complex regulations.
- **Proactivity**: Identifies risks before they result in violations or penalties.
- **Scalability**: Handles global compliance across multiple jurisdictions simultaneously.

Challenges:

- **Interpretation**: AI can track regulatory text, but human lawyers must interpret its legal and business implications.
- **Bias in Risk Scoring**: Algorithms may prioritize some risks incorrectly if trained on incomplete data.
- **Overreliance**: Companies may treat AI outputs as definitive, overlooking nuances that require legal expertise.
- **Data Security**: Compliance platforms themselves must be safeguarded, since they often process sensitive corporate information.

Key Takeaway

AI is transforming regulatory monitoring and compliance audits from slow, manual, and reactive processes into **dynamic, proactive safeguards**. By continuously scanning regulations, flagging risks, and automating audits, AI enables businesses to stay ahead of legal changes. Yet technology cannot replace the role of lawyers and compliance officers in interpreting laws, balancing risks, and ensuring that compliance is not just a box-ticking exercise but a driver of responsible business conduct.

Automating Anti-Money Laundering (AML) and Fraud Detection

Financial crime is one of the most pressing global challenges. Criminal networks launder an estimated **$2 trillion annually**, hiding illicit funds through complex financial systems. Banks, insurers, and other financial institutions face immense regulatory pressure to detect and prevent money laundering and fraud. Traditionally, compliance teams relied on manual checks and rule-based systems, which often generated overwhelming false positives. Today, **AI-**

driven solutions are reshaping AML and fraud detection, offering faster, more accurate, and proactive defenses.

The Traditional Struggle with AML

Historically, AML compliance has been **labor-intensive and reactive**:

- Rule-based systems flagged transactions over certain thresholds (e.g., large cash deposits).
- Compliance teams manually investigated alerts, often drowning in irrelevant results.
- Sophisticated criminals easily bypassed static rules by structuring transactions just below reporting thresholds.

The result: high compliance costs, frustrated regulators, and detection gaps that allowed illicit flows to continue.

How AI Transforms AML and Fraud Detection

AI leverages **machine learning, anomaly detection, and predictive analytics** to identify suspicious activity that traditional systems miss.

1. **Pattern Recognition** – AI can detect complex transaction patterns across accounts and jurisdictions, spotting hidden links between seemingly unrelated transfers.
2. **Adaptive Learning** – Unlike static rules, AI models evolve as criminals change tactics, continuously improving detection accuracy.
3. **Anomaly Detection** – AI identifies unusual behaviors, such as sudden spikes in transaction volume or transfers inconsistent with a customer's history.

4. **Network Analysis** – AI maps relationships between individuals, companies, and transactions to uncover hidden criminal networks.

Instead of overwhelming investigators with false positives, AI narrows alerts to the most suspicious cases, improving both efficiency and effectiveness.

Real-World Example: Fraud Prevention in Banking

A global bank deployed an AI-powered AML system to analyze millions of daily transactions. Traditional rule-based systems produced **90% false positives**. After integrating AI, false positives dropped dramatically, while actual fraud detection rates improved.

In another case, insurers used AI to spot fraudulent claims by analyzing behavioral data. For example, multiple claims filed from the same IP address or unusually fast claim submissions after a policy purchase were flagged as high-risk.

Opportunities and Challenges

Opportunities:

- **Regulatory Confidence**: Regulators increasingly expect advanced AI systems as part of robust AML programs.
- **Cost Efficiency**: Reduces time wasted on false positives.
- **Proactive Defense**: Detects sophisticated criminal strategies that evade traditional systems.
- **Global Scale**: Monitors vast transaction volumes across jurisdictions.

Challenges:

- **Bias and Errors**: AI models must be carefully trained to avoid unfairly flagging certain groups or transactions.
- **Transparency**: "Black box" AI models can be hard to explain to regulators demanding clear justification for flagged transactions.
- **Data Privacy**: Global AML monitoring often conflicts with local data protection laws, requiring careful legal balancing.
- **Overreliance**: Human oversight remains essential to interpret and validate AI findings.

Key Takeaway

AI is transforming AML and fraud detection from a reactive, rule-based exercise into a **dynamic, intelligent defense system**. By spotting hidden patterns, adapting to criminal behavior, and reducing false positives, AI not only improves compliance but also strengthens the global fight against financial crime. Yet, success depends on balance: leveraging machine intelligence while ensuring transparency, fairness, and human oversight in one of the most sensitive areas of legal compliance.

AI in GDPR, CCPA, and Global Privacy Compliance

Data has become the lifeblood of modern business, but with that power comes enormous responsibility. Regulations like the **General Data Protection Regulation (GDPR)** in Europe and the **California Consumer Privacy Act (CCPA)** in the U.S. set strict rules for how organizations collect, use, and share personal data. These laws are only the beginning—dozens of jurisdictions worldwide are enacting their own privacy frameworks. For companies operating globally, staying compliant is daunting. AI is now playing a crucial role in **monitoring, enforcing, and automating privacy compliance**.

The Complexity of Global Privacy Rules

GDPR and CCPA illustrate the diversity and complexity of modern privacy laws:

- **GDPR** emphasizes consent, data minimization, and the "right to be forgotten," with penalties of up to **4% of global revenue** for violations.
- **CCPA** grants California residents rights to access, delete, and opt out of the sale of personal data, with significant fines for breaches.
- Other countries, from Brazil (LGPD) to India and Japan, are enacting similar laws, each with unique requirements.

The challenge for businesses: complying with overlapping, sometimes conflicting rules across multiple jurisdictions, all while handling massive volumes of consumer data.

How AI Supports Privacy Compliance

AI systems can help organizations manage these obligations by:

1. **Data Mapping and Classification** – Identifying where personal data resides across servers, cloud systems, and devices, even when mislabeled or hidden.
2. **Consent Management** – Tracking and enforcing user preferences across platforms, ensuring that data is processed only with valid consent.

3. **Automated Rights Fulfillment** – Processing user requests under GDPR/CCPA, such as deleting personal data or providing access reports.
4. **Risk Detection** – Flagging risky data practices, such as excessive retention or sharing without proper safeguards.
5. **Cross-Border Compliance** – Monitoring international data transfers to ensure they comply with legal frameworks like the EU–U.S. Data Privacy Framework.

Real-World Example: Automated Data Subject Requests

Large tech companies receive **tens of thousands of data subject access requests (DSARs)** annually. Without automation, processing these requests would require enormous legal and IT resources. AI-powered compliance platforms can automatically locate relevant personal data, compile reports, and track deadlines, ensuring organizations meet GDPR's strict one-month response requirement.

Opportunities and Challenges

Opportunities:

- **Efficiency**: Automates compliance tasks that overwhelm human teams.
- **Accuracy**: Reduces the risk of human error in processing large datasets.
- **Global Reach**: Monitors multiple regulatory frameworks simultaneously.
- **Proactivity**: Flags risks before regulators or consumers raise complaints.

Challenges:

- **Dynamic Laws**: Regulations evolve rapidly; AI must adapt continuously.
- **Interpretation**: Legal teams still need to interpret vague concepts like "legitimate interest" or "reasonable security."
- **Overreliance on Automation**: Human oversight is essential to ensure fairness, especially when handling sensitive requests.
- **Data Security**: AI systems themselves must be protected from breaches, as they often handle vast amounts of personal data.

Key Takeaway

AI is becoming indispensable in managing GDPR, CCPA, and global privacy compliance. By automating data discovery, rights management, and risk detection, AI helps businesses stay compliant in a fast-changing regulatory landscape. But compliance is not just a technical exercise—it requires legal interpretation, ethical responsibility, and transparent communication with consumers. The most successful organizations will combine AI efficiency with a culture of privacy and accountability.

Corporate Governance and Risk Management Through AI

Strong corporate governance is the backbone of sustainable business. Boards of directors and executives are expected to oversee compliance, manage risks, and ensure long-term accountability to shareholders, regulators, and society at large. In an era of increasing complexity and scrutiny, **AI is becoming an essential tool** for strengthening governance and managing risk. By offering real-time insights, predictive analytics, and automated oversight, AI enables leaders to make better-informed decisions and avoid blind spots that could harm the organization.

The Governance Challenge

Modern corporations face governance challenges on multiple fronts:

- **Regulatory Expectations**: Directors are personally accountable for compliance failures.
- **Shareholder Demands**: Investors push for transparency on environmental, social, and governance (ESG) issues.
- **Operational Complexity**: Multinational companies must manage risks across global operations, from supply chains to cybersecurity.
- **Reputational Risks**: Social media amplifies the impact of governance failures, turning small missteps into public crises.

Boards cannot rely solely on periodic reports—they need continuous visibility into emerging risks.

How AI Enhances Corporate Governance

AI technologies help governance bodies by:

1. **Risk Monitoring** – Continuously scanning internal and external data sources to detect potential legal, financial, or reputational risks.
2. **Predictive Analytics** – Forecasting potential crises, such as regulatory investigations, supply chain disruptions, or cyberattacks.
3. **Board Decision Support** – Summarizing complex legal and compliance information into actionable dashboards.

4. **Policy Compliance** – Ensuring company policies are consistently applied and flagging deviations in real time.
5. **ESG Oversight** – Analyzing sustainability data, diversity metrics, and corporate disclosures to help boards meet growing ESG reporting requirements.

AI in Risk Management

Risk management is no longer about identifying issues after they occur—it is about predicting and mitigating them before they escalate. AI enables:

- **Financial Risk Detection**: Spotting irregular accounting patterns that may signal fraud.
- **Cybersecurity Risk Analysis**: Identifying vulnerabilities and predicting potential breaches.
- **Operational Risk Tracking**: Monitoring supply chains for instability, such as vendors in regions prone to political unrest.
- **Legal Risk Alerts**: Flagging contracts or practices likely to trigger regulatory scrutiny.

This proactive approach shifts risk management from defensive to strategic, giving companies a competitive advantage.

Real-World Example: AI in Boardrooms

Some companies are integrating AI-driven dashboards into board meetings. These systems aggregate real-time data on compliance, litigation exposure, ESG performance, and reputational risks. Instead of relying on static quarterly reports, directors can see live risk indicators—allowing faster, more informed governance decisions.

For instance, if an AI system detects unusual trading patterns suggesting insider risk, the board can act immediately, reducing potential liability and reputational damage.

Opportunities and Challenges

Opportunities:

- **Transparency**: Provides boards with a clearer, real-time view of organizational health.
- **Accountability**: Strengthens compliance and reduces regulatory exposure.
- **Efficiency**: Automates oversight, freeing directors to focus on strategy.
- **Stakeholder Trust**: Demonstrates a commitment to responsible, data-driven governance.

Challenges:

- **Overreliance on Technology**: Directors must avoid treating AI outputs as unquestionable.
- **Bias and Inaccuracy**: AI insights are only as good as the data feeding them.
- **Explainability**: Boards must be able to justify decisions to regulators and shareholders, which requires transparency in AI models.
- **Ethical Concerns**: Balancing efficiency with fairness, especially in areas like workforce monitoring.

Key Takeaway

AI is reshaping corporate governance and risk management, offering leaders unprecedented visibility and foresight. By automating monitoring, predicting crises, and strengthening compliance, AI helps boards fulfill their fiduciary duties with greater confidence. Still, governance is not just about data—it is about judgment, accountability, and trust. AI can illuminate the path, but human leaders must walk it with integrity.

CHAPTER 7

Ethical, Social, and Legal Challenges

Bias and Discrimination in AI Legal Systems

One of the greatest promises of AI in law is its ability to process data objectively, free from human emotion or prejudice. Yet reality tells a different story. AI systems are not neutral—they inherit biases from the data on which they are trained and the human choices that shape their design. In the legal field, where fairness and equality are foundational principles, biased AI can create outcomes that undermine justice rather than enhance it.

How Bias Enters Legal AI

Bias in AI does not appear out of thin air. It arises from several sources:

1. **Historical Data** – If past legal decisions reflect systemic bias (e.g., harsher sentencing for minority groups), AI models trained on this data will reproduce those disparities.
2. **Imbalanced Datasets** – If training data lacks diversity, the system may fail to account for the experiences of underrepresented groups.
3. **Design Choices** – Developers decide what data to include, how to label it, and what outcomes to prioritize—choices that inevitably reflect human judgment.
4. **Feedback Loops** – AI systems deployed in real-world environments can reinforce existing patterns, creating a cycle of discrimination.

For example, an AI bail recommendation tool might consistently rate defendants from certain neighborhoods as "high risk," not because of individual behavior but because of correlations in biased historical policing data.

Real-World Examples of Bias in Legal AI

- **U.S. Criminal Justice**: The COMPAS risk assessment tool, used to guide sentencing and parole decisions, was found to disproportionately classify Black defendants as higher risk of reoffending compared to white defendants, even when actual reoffense rates were lower.
- **Hiring and Employment**: AI systems screening resumes for law firm positions have been shown to replicate biases against candidates from nontraditional schools or minority backgrounds if trained on past hiring data.
- **Predictive Policing**: Some AI tools direct police resources to neighborhoods historically associated with crime, perpetuating over-policing in marginalized communities.

These cases highlight the danger of assuming that AI is inherently fair.

Ethical and Legal Implications

Bias in legal AI is not just a technical flaw—it is a threat to fundamental rights:

- **Equality Before the Law**: Biased systems undermine the principle that justice must be impartial.
- **Due Process**: If AI recommendations influence judicial decisions, defendants must have the right to challenge the basis of those algorithms.
- **Transparency and Accountability**: Without explainability, it is nearly impossible to detect or correct biased outcomes.

Governments and regulators are increasingly scrutinizing AI in law. The EU's **AI Act**, for example, classifies AI used in justice systems as "high risk," requiring strict oversight and transparency.

Mitigating Bias in Legal AI

Solutions exist, though none are simple:

1. **Diverse Training Data** – Incorporating data that reflects a broad range of populations and contexts.
2. **Bias Audits** – Regular independent reviews to detect and correct discriminatory patterns.
3. **Explainable AI** – Designing systems whose decision-making processes can be understood and scrutinized.
4. **Human Oversight** – Ensuring that AI outputs are advisory, not determinative, with final decisions made by accountable legal professionals.

For example, an AI system that predicts case outcomes could present not only probabilities but also the key factors driving its analysis, enabling lawyers and judges to critically assess its recommendations.

Key Takeaway

AI has the power to enhance fairness by removing some human biases—but only if designed and deployed responsibly. Left unchecked, AI risks **amplifying existing inequities** and undermining trust in the justice system. The path forward lies in transparency, accountability, and human oversight. AI should serve as a tool to support justice, never as a substitute for it.

Data Privacy and Client Confidentiality Risks

Confidentiality is the cornerstone of the lawyer–client relationship. Clients share sensitive information with the expectation that it will remain protected, both ethically and legally. The rise of AI in law introduces powerful new capabilities—but also new risks to privacy and confidentiality. From cloud-based research tools to AI-driven contract analysis, sensitive client data is increasingly processed, stored, and analyzed by machines. Ensuring that these technologies respect confidentiality is one of the most pressing ethical challenges facing the legal profession today.

Why Confidentiality Matters in Law

Confidentiality is not merely a professional courtesy; it is an ethical obligation enshrined in rules of professional conduct worldwide. Breaches of confidentiality can:

- Undermine client trust.
- Compromise litigation strategies.
- Expose sensitive business or personal information to competitors or adversaries.
- Result in disciplinary action or liability for lawyers and firms.

In the digital era, confidentiality risks extend far beyond a misplaced file or overheard conversation.

AI's Privacy Risks

AI systems introduce new vulnerabilities at multiple levels:

1. **Data Input Risks** – Sensitive information may be entered into AI platforms hosted on third-party servers. Without safeguards, this data could be exposed or reused for model training.
2. **Cloud Storage** – Many AI tools store data remotely. If security is inadequate, breaches could reveal confidential documents.
3. **Cross-Border Transfers** – Data processed by AI may move across jurisdictions, triggering conflicting privacy laws (e.g., GDPR vs. U.S. discovery obligations).
4. **Model Leakage** – Improperly designed generative AI models may inadvertently "remember" and reproduce confidential information entered by users.
5. **Cybersecurity Vulnerabilities** – AI systems are attractive targets for hackers due to the volume of sensitive data they process.

Real-World Example: Generative AI Risks

In 2023, several law firms restricted the use of generative AI platforms after concerns arose that uploading client documents could compromise confidentiality. If a lawyer uses a public AI tool to draft a contract or summarize litigation documents, there is a risk that proprietary client data becomes part of the model's training corpus, accessible in unintended ways.

This illustrates the tension between embracing efficiency and safeguarding the ethical duty of confidentiality.

Mitigating Privacy and Confidentiality Risks

Lawyers and firms can adopt multiple safeguards to balance innovation with responsibility:

1. **Private AI Models** – Deploy AI systems within secure, firm-controlled environments rather than public platforms.
2. **Data Minimization** – Limit the amount of client information shared with AI tools, stripping out identifiers where possible.
3. **Encryption and Security** – Ensure all data processed by AI is encrypted both in transit and at rest.
4. **Vendor Due Diligence** – Evaluate AI providers for compliance with privacy regulations and contractual confidentiality guarantees.
5. **Ethical Training** – Educate lawyers on responsible AI use, reinforcing that ethical duties do not change with technology.

Regulatory and Legal Oversight

Privacy laws intersect with confidentiality obligations in complex ways. Regulations like GDPR and CCPA impose strict requirements on how personal data is handled, while professional conduct rules demand heightened protection for client information. Bar associations and regulators are now issuing guidance on AI use, emphasizing that **lawyers remain ultimately accountable** for protecting client confidentiality, regardless of the tools they employ.

Key Takeaway

AI offers enormous opportunities for efficiency and insight, but it also magnifies the risks of breaching client confidentiality and data privacy. Lawyers must treat AI as an extension of their ethical responsibilities, applying the same diligence to machine use as they would to human assistants. Trust is the currency of law—and without robust safeguards, AI risks devaluing it.

The Debate on "AI Lawyers": Unauthorized Practice of Law?

One of the most provocative questions in legal ethics is whether AI systems can—or should—act as lawyers. Already, AI-powered platforms draft contracts, answer legal questions, and even provide courtroom guidance to self-represented litigants. While these tools expand access to justice, they also raise a pressing concern: **are AI systems engaging in the unauthorized practice of law (UPL)?**

What Counts as Practicing Law?

The definition of "practicing law" varies across jurisdictions, but generally includes:

- Giving legal advice tailored to an individual's situation.
- Drafting legally binding documents.
- Representing parties in court.

Under this standard, an AI system that merely provides general legal information (e.g., explaining what a lease is) is not practicing law. But an AI that advises a tenant on how to challenge an eviction, or drafts a personalized will, may cross the line into UPL.

The Case of AI Legal Tools

Recent years have seen a surge in AI-driven legal products:

- **Chatbots** that guide individuals through filing small claims or contesting traffic tickets.
- **Contract generators** that draft customized agreements for startups.
- **Virtual assistants** that help employees answer compliance questions.

These tools often operate in a gray zone. On the one hand, they democratize legal access by helping people who cannot afford a lawyer. On the other hand, regulators worry they may mislead users, provide inaccurate advice, or undermine consumer protections.

Real-World Example: DoNotPay

In 2023, the startup **DoNotPay**—branded as "the world's first robot lawyer"—faced lawsuits alleging unauthorized practice of law. While the company claimed to empower consumers to handle simple legal tasks, critics argued its AI was effectively giving legal advice without proper licensing or oversight.

This case highlights the tension between innovation and regulation: should AI tools be restricted to protect consumers, or embraced to expand access to justice?

Ethical and Legal Implications

The debate over AI lawyers touches on fundamental issues:

- **Consumer Protection**: Without licensing or regulation, how can users be sure AI advice is accurate and reliable?
- **Access to Justice**: Millions lack affordable legal representation. Should AI tools be barred if they provide meaningful assistance?
- **Professional Boundaries**: If AI can handle routine tasks, how should the legal profession redefine its role?
- **Accountability**: Who is responsible if AI advice causes harm—the developer, the platform, or the user?

Potential Paths Forward

Solutions are beginning to emerge:

1. **Regulatory Sandboxes** – Some jurisdictions allow AI legal tools to operate in controlled environments, testing innovation while protecting consumers.
2. **Certification Systems** – AI tools could be certified by regulatory bodies to ensure accuracy and reliability.
3. **Hybrid Models** – AI tools may assist with routine tasks but require human lawyer oversight for personalized advice.
4. **Redefining Legal Services** – The profession may need to distinguish between legal "information" (which AI can provide) and legal "advice" (which requires a licensed professional).

Key Takeaway

The rise of AI in law is forcing a reexamination of what it means to "practice law." While fears of AI replacing lawyers may be overstated, the risk of unauthorized practice is real—and regulators must strike a balance between protecting consumers and enabling innovation. The most promising path lies in **hybrid approaches** where AI expands access to justice under responsible oversight, ensuring technology strengthens rather than undermines the rule of law.

Accountability, Liability, and Trust in AI-Driven Legal Decisions

The use of AI in legal practice raises a fundamental question: **who is responsible when AI makes a mistake?** In law, where decisions affect rights, freedoms, and livelihoods, accountability cannot be vague. Whether AI is used to predict case outcomes, recommend sentences, or draft contracts, errors are inevitable. The challenge is determining **who bears liability**—the lawyer, the firm, the client, or the AI developer—and how to maintain trust in a justice system increasingly shaped by algorithms.

The Accountability Dilemma

Traditionally, accountability in law is clear: lawyers are responsible for their advice, judges for their rulings, and firms for their procedures. With AI, the chain of responsibility becomes more complicated:

- If a lawyer relies on an AI tool that produces an incorrect case citation, is the lawyer negligent?

- If an AI bail assessment algorithm wrongly labels a defendant as high-risk, who is accountable—the judge who used it, or the company that built it?
- If a firm integrates AI into compliance monitoring but fails to catch violations, can regulators hold both the firm and the vendor responsible?

Without clear answers, accountability risks being diluted, undermining both legal ethics and public confidence.

Liability in AI Legal Systems

Courts and regulators are beginning to explore liability frameworks:

1. **Lawyer Liability** – Lawyers remain ultimately responsible for verifying AI outputs. Courts have sanctioned attorneys who submitted briefs containing AI-generated but fabricated citations.
2. **Vendor Liability** – Developers of AI tools may face liability if their products are negligently designed, misleading, or marketed as foolproof.
3. **Shared Responsibility** – Increasingly, accountability may be distributed, with lawyers, firms, and AI providers sharing liability for errors.
4. **Regulatory Standards** – Laws like the EU's proposed AI Act classify legal AI as "high risk," requiring strict compliance with transparency, testing, and oversight obligations.

The Trust Factor

Liability is not just a legal issue—it is about trust. For clients to embrace AI-assisted law, they must believe:

- Their information is secure.
- AI recommendations are reliable.
- Humans remain in control of critical judgments.

Trust is especially fragile in justice systems. If people believe outcomes are determined by opaque algorithms rather than transparent reasoning, confidence in the rule of law could erode.

Building Trustworthy AI in Law

To ensure accountability and trust, several measures are emerging:

- **Explainability**: AI systems must provide transparent reasoning for their outputs, not just answers.
- **Auditability**: Independent audits of AI tools can verify fairness, accuracy, and compliance.
- **Human Oversight**: Lawyers and judges must remain the ultimate decision-makers, using AI as an aid, not a substitute.
- **Clear Liability Rules**: Legislators and bar associations must define responsibility to prevent accountability gaps.

For example, an AI case prediction tool might show not just that a motion has a "70% chance of success," but also the factors driving that probability—judge history, case facts, and legal arguments. This transparency builds confidence in both the tool and the lawyer using it.

Key Takeaway

AI can improve accuracy and efficiency in law, but without clear accountability, liability, and transparency, trust in both technology and the justice system will erode. The future of AI in law depends on balancing innovation with responsibility: ensuring that when mistakes occur, accountability is clear, liability is fair, and trust in justice is preserved. AI may assist decision-making, but humans must remain the guardians of legal integrity.

CHAPTER 8

The Future of AI in Law

The Evolving Role of Human Lawyers in an AI-Powered Profession

For centuries, the role of lawyers has remained largely unchanged: interpreting laws, advising clients, drafting documents, and advocating in court. The arrival of AI does not eliminate these functions, but it is **reshaping how they are performed**. Routine tasks that once consumed hours—legal research, document review, contract drafting—can now be completed by machines in minutes. This transformation raises a profound question: **what will the lawyer of the future do?**

From Information Gatekeepers to Strategic Advisors

In the past, lawyers were prized for their ability to access and process legal information. With AI systems now able to sift through vast databases in seconds, the value of lawyers is shifting. Clients no longer pay for access to information—they pay for **interpretation, strategy, and judgment**.

Future lawyers will be less like information gatekeepers and more like **trusted advisors** who:

- Translate AI insights into meaningful legal strategies.
- Balance efficiency with ethics and fairness.
- Provide human empathy and persuasion that machines cannot replicate.

The Human Skills Machines Cannot Replace

AI may master data analysis, but several uniquely human skills remain irreplaceable:

1. **Judgment** – Deciding which risks are acceptable based on context, strategy, and client goals.
2. **Ethical Reasoning** – Weighing not just what is legal but what is fair and just.
3. **Advocacy and Persuasion** – Crafting arguments that resonate with human judges and juries.
4. **Empathy** – Building trust with clients in moments of vulnerability or crisis.
5. **Creativity** – Designing novel arguments or innovative deal structures outside established patterns.

AI can inform these functions, but it cannot perform them independently.

Lawyers as AI Managers

Another critical role for lawyers will be **AI management**—selecting, supervising, and validating AI tools. Just as junior associates were once trained to review documents under supervision, AI tools must be monitored to ensure accuracy and fairness. Lawyers will increasingly act as:

- **Curators of Technology** – Choosing AI systems that align with client needs and ethical obligations.
- **Validators** – Checking outputs for errors, bias, or misinterpretation.
- **Translators** – Explaining AI-generated insights to clients and courts in clear, understandable terms.

Real-World Example: AI in Litigation Strategy

A law firm might use AI to predict case outcomes, identifying a 65% chance of success on a motion to dismiss. But only the lawyer can interpret whether pursuing the motion aligns with client strategy— balancing cost, business reputation, and long-term goals. The AI provides probabilities; the lawyer provides judgment.

Opportunities and Risks for Lawyers

Opportunities:

- Lawyers can focus more on high-value tasks such as negotiation, advocacy, and client counseling.
- Smaller firms gain access to tools that level the playing field with large firms.
- Lawyers with tech fluency will find new career paths in **legal tech consulting** and **AI ethics advisory roles**.

Risks:

- Lawyers who resist AI may be left behind as clients demand faster, cheaper services.
- Overreliance on AI could weaken critical legal skills if not balanced with training and practice.
- Ethical risks remain if lawyers fail to supervise AI outputs properly.

Key Takeaway

AI is not replacing lawyers—it is **redefining them**. The lawyers of the future will spend less time searching for answers and more time interpreting, advising, and advocating. Their greatest value will lie not in competing with machines, but in mastering the uniquely human skills—judgment, ethics, creativity, and empathy—that no algorithm can replicate. The AI-powered profession belongs not to lawyers who fear change, but to those who embrace it as a partner in delivering justice.

New Career Paths: Legal Technologists and AI Ethics Advisors

The rise of AI in law is not just transforming existing roles—it is creating **entirely new career paths**. As technology becomes central to legal practice, firms and institutions need professionals who can bridge the gap between law and AI. Two of the most prominent emerging roles are **legal technologists** and **AI ethics advisors**. These positions reflect a growing recognition that future legal services will be built not only on statutes and precedents, but also on algorithms and ethical frameworks.

The Legal Technologist

A legal technologist is part lawyer, part data scientist, and part strategist. Their mission is to help firms and clients leverage technology responsibly and effectively.

Core responsibilities include:

- Selecting and implementing AI tools for research, contract review, compliance, and litigation support.
- Training legal teams to use new technologies.
- Working with developers to ensure AI systems reflect legal standards and practical needs.
- Designing workflows that integrate AI seamlessly into client service.

For example, a legal technologist might oversee the deployment of an AI-powered due diligence platform in a merger, ensuring it extracts the right contractual risks while aligning with confidentiality obligations.

Why this role matters: As clients demand efficiency and transparency, firms with strong legal technologists will have a competitive edge.

The AI Ethics Advisor

While legal technologists focus on **how** AI is used, AI ethics advisors focus on **whether it should be used—and how to do so responsibly**.

Core responsibilities include:

- Auditing AI systems for bias, discrimination, or privacy violations.
- Advising firms on regulatory compliance with emerging AI laws (such as the EU AI Act).
- Developing internal policies for ethical AI use.
- Acting as a liaison between law firms, regulators, and clients on questions of trust and accountability.

For example, an ethics advisor might evaluate whether a predictive sentencing tool used in criminal justice unfairly disadvantages minority groups, and recommend safeguards before deployment.

Why this role matters: As AI becomes more embedded in justice systems, public trust depends on ensuring that automation does not compromise fairness or rights.

Other Emerging Roles in the AI-Legal Ecosystem

- **Legal Data Analysts** – Specialists who interpret large datasets for litigation or regulatory strategy.
- **Legal Operations Managers** – Professionals who streamline workflows by integrating AI into billing, staffing, and case management.
- **AI Policy Consultants** – Experts advising governments and organizations on crafting AI-related laws and policies.

These roles demonstrate that the future of law is increasingly interdisciplinary, requiring collaboration between lawyers, technologists, and ethicists.

Real-World Example: Law Firms Hiring Technologists

Leading firms are already recruiting **chief innovation officers** and **AI project managers**. Some firms now maintain in-house "legal labs" where lawyers and technologists co-develop tools for contract automation, compliance, and client dashboards. Similarly, bar associations and universities are offering new certifications and degrees in legal technology and AI ethics, signaling the institutional recognition of these career paths.

Opportunities and Challenges

Opportunities:

- Expands career options beyond traditional practice.
- Positions legal professionals at the forefront of technological innovation.
- Enhances client trust through transparent, ethical AI practices.

- Strengthens collaboration between law, technology, and business.

Challenges:

- Requires retraining and continuous learning in technology and data science.
- Risk of resistance from traditionalists who view these roles as peripheral.
- The legal profession must develop standards and accreditation for these new specialties.

Key Takeaway

AI is not just changing *how* lawyers work—it is changing *who* lawyers can become. Legal technologists and AI ethics advisors represent the future of the profession, where law meets innovation and ethics. These roles will shape not only how firms compete but also how justice systems maintain fairness and trust in an AI-driven world. Lawyers who embrace these new paths will not just adapt to change—they will lead it.

The Vision of Fully Automated Legal Systems: Realistic or Dystopian?

The idea of a fully automated legal system—where disputes are resolved, contracts executed, and judgments delivered entirely by machines—has fascinated technologists and alarmed legal professionals in equal measure. On one hand, automation promises efficiency, speed, and reduced costs. On the other, it raises profound concerns about fairness, accountability, and the very essence of justice. The question is not just whether such systems are possible, but whether they are desirable.

The Allure of Full Automation

Advocates of automation highlight several potential benefits:

- **Efficiency**: Automated systems could process disputes at scale, reducing court backlogs.
- **Cost Reduction**: Eliminating manual processes could make justice affordable and accessible to all.
- **Consistency**: Algorithms could deliver uniform application of laws, reducing human subjectivity.
- **Transparency**: Digital systems could provide clear audit trails of every decision.

In theory, an automated court could hear millions of small claims in seconds, freeing human judges to focus on complex disputes. Similarly, automated contract execution could remove delays and disputes caused by human error.

The Risks of a Machine-Driven Justice

Yet, the dystopian vision is equally powerful. Fully automated legal systems risk:

1. **Dehumanization of Justice** – Law is not only about rules; it is about fairness, empathy, and moral reasoning. A system without human judgment could miss the human impact of decisions.
2. **Bias Amplification** – AI trained on biased data may reproduce or even amplify systemic discrimination.
3. **Opacity** – Many AI models operate as "black boxes," making it difficult to explain why a decision was made.
4. **Erosion of Trust** – Citizens may lose faith in a justice system perceived as cold, mechanical, or unchallengeable.
5. **Accountability Gaps** – If an algorithm delivers an unjust ruling, who is responsible—the judge, the developer, or the machine itself?

These risks suggest that a fully automated system could undermine the very values it seeks to uphold.

Real-World Experiments

Some jurisdictions are already experimenting with automation:

- **Estonia** piloted an AI "judge" for small claims disputes under €7,000, where parties could contest the decision before a human judge.
- **China** has developed "smart courts" that automate parts of case management, evidence handling, and even draft judgments.
- **Online Dispute Resolution (ODR)** platforms in the U.S. and EU use algorithms to settle consumer and e-commerce disputes without human arbitrators.

These initiatives suggest that automation is feasible—but only for specific, low-stakes areas where efficiency outweighs the need for nuanced judgment.

A More Likely Future: Hybrid Justice

The future of legal systems is unlikely to be fully automated or purely human. Instead, we are moving toward **hybrid justice models**, where AI handles routine, high-volume tasks while humans retain authority over complex or high-stakes decisions.

For example:

- AI might triage cases, recommend settlements, or draft judgments.
- Human judges would review, refine, or overturn AI-generated recommendations.
- Lawyers would interpret AI findings for clients, ensuring fairness and accountability.

This partnership preserves efficiency while maintaining the human values essential to justice.

Key Takeaway

A fully automated legal system may sound efficient, but it risks turning justice into a mechanical process devoid of fairness and empathy. The more realistic—and desirable—future is hybrid: **AI as an assistant, not a replacement.** By letting machines handle scale and speed while humans safeguard ethics and interpretation, legal systems can harness technology without sacrificing legitimacy. The choice is not between realistic or dystopian—it is about designing a future where AI strengthens justice rather than undermines it.

Preparing Legal Professionals for the AI-Driven Future

The legal profession stands at a crossroads. AI is no longer an emerging experiment—it is a present reality shaping research, contracts, litigation, compliance, and governance. For lawyers, judges, regulators, and students, the question is not whether AI will transform law, but **how to prepare for that transformation**. The future belongs to those who adapt, embrace continuous learning, and cultivate skills that machines cannot replicate.

Rethinking Legal Education

Law schools have traditionally emphasized case law, statutes, and doctrinal analysis. While these foundations remain critical, the next generation of lawyers must also understand:

- **Legal Technology** – How AI tools operate, their capabilities, and their limits.
- **Data Literacy** – How to interpret datasets, assess probabilities, and identify risks.
- **Ethics in AI** – How to balance efficiency with fairness, transparency, and accountability.

Some forward-looking institutions now offer courses in legal tech, coding for lawyers, and AI ethics. Bar associations are also updating continuing legal education (CLE) requirements to include technological competence.

Building Interdisciplinary Skills

The lawyer of the future is not just a legal expert—they are a **bridge-builder** between law, technology, and business. Key interdisciplinary skills include:

- **Collaboration with Technologists** – Working with AI developers to ensure legal tools meet real-world needs.
- **Policy and Regulation Expertise** – Advising on how AI should be regulated to balance innovation and risk.
- **Business Strategy** – Using AI insights to provide not just legal advice but competitive advantage for clients.

For example, an in-house lawyer advising a global corporation may need to integrate legal, technological, and business considerations when deploying AI for compliance monitoring.

Lifelong Learning and Adaptability

AI evolves rapidly—what is cutting-edge today may be obsolete tomorrow. Legal professionals must commit to **lifelong learning**. This means:

- Regularly updating knowledge of AI tools.
- Staying current on emerging regulations such as the EU AI Act.
- Participating in professional networks and innovation forums.

Adaptability will be as important as legal expertise. Lawyers who thrive will be those willing to experiment, learn, and pivot as new technologies emerge.

Preserving the Human Core of Law

While AI transforms processes, the **human dimension of law remains irreplaceable**. Lawyers must double down on skills that AI cannot provide:

- Empathy in client relationships.
- Judgment in weighing legal, ethical, and strategic factors.
- Persuasion in negotiations and courtrooms.
- Integrity in upholding justice and trust.

In fact, as machines take over routine tasks, the human core of law will become even more central—because clients will value human judgment precisely where AI cannot reach.

Real-World Example: The Future-Ready Law Firm

Some law firms already position themselves as "AI-enabled advisors." They combine automated research, contract review, and litigation prediction with human-led strategy sessions, ensuring that clients get both efficiency and insight. These firms invest in **training programs, innovation labs, and cross-disciplinary teams**, signaling a model for the profession at large.

Key Takeaway

Preparing for the AI-driven future is not about competing with machines—it is about complementing them. Legal professionals must cultivate technological literacy, interdisciplinary expertise, and lifelong adaptability, while preserving the uniquely human values that define law. The lawyers who succeed will not be those who resist AI, but those who **master the art of partnership with it**, ensuring that technology strengthens—not supplants—the principles of justice.

Glossary of Key Terms

AI (Artificial Intelligence): Computer systems designed to perform tasks that typically require human intelligence, such as reasoning, learning, and decision-making.

Algorithm: A set of rules or instructions a computer follows to solve problems or make decisions.

Alternative Dispute Resolution (ADR): Methods of resolving legal disputes outside of court, such as mediation and arbitration.

Anomaly Detection: An AI technique used to identify unusual patterns in data that may indicate fraud, errors, or risks.

Automated Case Analysis: The use of AI to quickly process and interpret case law or statutes to identify relevant precedents.

Bias in AI: Systematic errors in AI outputs caused by skewed or unrepresentative training data, often leading to unfair or discriminatory results.

Blockchain: A decentralized, secure digital ledger used to record transactions, often forming the foundation for smart contracts.

Case Relevance Ranking: An AI-driven process that orders legal cases based on their importance or applicability to a given matter.

Compliance Monitoring: The use of technology to track organizational adherence to laws, regulations, and internal policies.

Data Privacy: The protection of personal or sensitive information from unauthorized access or misuse.

E-Discovery (Electronic Discovery): The process of identifying, collecting, and analyzing electronically stored information for use in litigation or investigation.

Generative AI: AI that can create new content, such as text, images, or documents, based on training data and user prompts.

Legal Technologist: A professional who integrates technology into legal services, helping firms and clients adopt and manage AI tools.

Machine Learning (ML): A subset of AI where systems learn from data and improve their performance without being explicitly programmed.

Natural Language Processing (NLP): AI technology that enables machines to understand, interpret, and generate human language.

Predictive Analytics: The use of AI to forecast outcomes based on historical data patterns, such as predicting case results.

Redlining: The process of comparing contract drafts to highlight changes, additions, and deletions.

Smart Contracts: Self-executing agreements stored on blockchain that automatically enforce terms when conditions are met.

Stare Decisis: A legal principle requiring courts to follow established precedent in similar cases.

Unauthorized Practice of Law (UPL): The provision of legal advice or services by someone who is not licensed to practice law, a concern now raised by AI legal tools.

Virtual Courtroom: A digital environment where legal proceedings are conducted remotely using video conferencing and AI-enhanced tools.

Thank You

Thank you for joining us on this journey through the evolving landscape of **AI in law**. This book was written with one purpose in mind: to help lawyers, students, business leaders, and policymakers understand both the opportunities and challenges AI brings to the legal profession.

The future of law is not about machines replacing humans—it is about **humans and machines working together** to create a more efficient, accessible, and just system. AI will continue to change how lawyers research, draft, negotiate, and advocate, but the core values of the profession—**judgment, integrity, empathy, and fairness**—will remain firmly human.

By engaging with these ideas, you are already preparing for the next chapter of legal practice. Whether you are a lawyer, technologist, or client, your role in shaping this transformation is vital.

If this book has sparked insights, challenged your perspective, or helped you prepare for the future, we would be deeply grateful if you shared your thoughts in an **Amazon review**. Your feedback not only supports this work but also helps other readers discover it and join the conversation about the future of AI in law.

On behalf of everyone who contributed to this work, thank you for your time, your curiosity, and your commitment to building a legal profession ready for the AI-driven future.

Eric LeBouthillier

www.ingramcontent.com/pod-product-compliance
Lightning Source LLC
Chambersburg PA
CBHW071711210326
41597CB00017B/2428